WHAT A CHRISTIAN BELIEVES AND WHY

BY

C. F. HUNTER

Author of

"The New Testament : Its Writers and Their Messages,"
"The Life History of the New Testament,"
"An Introduction to Sunday School Work," etc,

NEW AND REVISED EDITION

LONDON:
METHODIST YOUTH DEPARTMENT,
LUDGATE CIRCUS HOUSE, E.C.4

Printed and bound in Great Britain by
The Hollen Street Press, Ltd., London, W.1

PREFACE

IT is now twenty years since this book was first written ; and it is very gratifying to find that it is still meeting a definite need both at home and on the mission field, where it has been translated into several languages. Hitherto it has been reprinted each time from the original plates, but it has been felt desirable now to reset it in more modern form and issue it at a lower price.

I have taken the opportunity to revise it so far as may be necessary ; and Professor Henry Bett, M.A., Litt.D., of Handsworth College, Birmingham, a theologian of profound learning and very sound judgment, has done me the great kindness of reading it with that end in view. He has made a few very helpful suggestions, but the alterations and additions are not numerous, and leaders of classes will find no difficulty where some of their students have the old edition and others the new.

A phrase has been altered here and there, and in view of the events of the last twenty years and the present condition of Europe, pp. 63—64 have been rewritten. Additional matter of some importance will be found on: p. 10, the derivation of "Agnostic"; p. 43, "Persons" in the Trinity ; p. 105, self-consciousness ; p. 106, paragraph (f) ; p. 136, the Greek Church ; p. 178, Time in relation to spiritual existence.

To meet war-time regulations the book has been reset in another type, but there is no change in the contents except in the paging.

C. F. H.

July, 1945.

CONTENTS

iv

CONTENTS

CHAPTER V

CHAPTER VI

CHAPTER VII

CHAPTER VIII

CHAPTER IX

CHAPTER X

CHAPTER XI

CHAPTER XII

CHAPTER I

WHY WE BELIEVE IN GOD

THEOLOGY means the word or teaching about God, and seeks to arrange in order our fragments of knowledge concerning God, Man and Religion. We shall, therefore, make our beginning with the subject of GOD.

The simplest and most convincing reasons for our belief in God may be arranged under three heads:

A. The belief is so universal as to be almost an instinct in Man.

B. The World in which we live compels us to believe in a Creator.

C. Our Consciences testify to a God to whom we are responsible.

A.—THE UNIVERSAL INSTINCT

Few books are richer in variety and interest than well-written records of travel. But whilst our travellers and explorers have to tell of races differing from our own in appearance, colour and speech, in food, dwellings and dress, in occupations and habits, in legends and traditions, yet *every race* has this in common with our own, that it has a Religion of some kind. The conception of God may be crude or even revolting, but every missionary has this as a starting-point, that those to whom he speaks are familiar with the idea of one or more Unseen Beings.

In the same way, the study of History, however far we may carry it back, makes it clear that in *every age* men have cherished this belief in gods, one or many, and that it has been one of the most important influences in shaping the life both of individuals and of nations.

1

Many see in this universal belief a reason for saying that there must be a real God to explain it. It is true that there have been widespread beliefs, such as the belief in witchcraft, that have proved false and have been discarded with the progress of knowledge. But in this case no advance of knowledge or civilization permanently weakens the conviction or makes men feel less need of God. It is so far an instinct that those who abandon it have to make an effort to do so, and probably never quite escape from it, as is shown by the fact that in the great crises of life avowed unbelievers have often turned to prayer in spite of their denial of God. The nobler-minded unbeliever is always conscious of loss, and sometimes has a pathetic sense of unsatisfied longing for something to take the place of God. The baser kind of unbeliever, too, who boasts that he fears neither God nor man nor devil, has his moments when he is not so sure that there is no God to be reckoned with.

The belief in God is so universal, so persistent, and so instinctive, that it can hardly be a delusion.

B.—THE WORLD WE LIVE IN

If this belief is true, it is obvious that we may expect to find confirmation of it in the World around us. In our attempts to read the story of its origin, we reach three conclusions:

1. The World was created in Time ;
2. Created by an Intelligent Being ;
3. Created with a Purpose.

There are three questions continually on the tongue of the little child: When? How? Why? All the knowledge and science of a later growth consists of attempts to answer similar questions concerning the Universe, and especially concerning the particular World in which we find ourselves.

1. *Origin in time.* The first question is, *When did this World come into existence?* It is clear that, in the form in which we know it, it cannot always have existed: the rocks tell the story of its development ; other worlds can be seen in the making and in decay ; and it is the verdict

equally of Science and of the Bible that in the beginning "the earth was waste and void," or, as Science puts it, a whirling mass of fire-mist. For our present purpose, it is of little importance whether Matter, the raw material, is supposed to be eternal or not: that is a deeper question, which does not touch the present argument, and must be left for larger and more learned books than this. The fact of real importance is rather that the solid World we see is *a made thing*, with a definite beginning in Time, and must have had a Cause or Maker.

The answer to the question *When?* is, therefore, that:

The World had a beginning, no matter how far back, and there must have been One existing before it, who could be its Maker.

2. *The Work of an Intelligent Creator.* The second question is, *How did the World come into existence?* The World did not make itself. It has, indeed, been argued that it might have come into being by a kind of chance—that the untold billions of atoms in the whirling fire-mist jostling one another formed larger groups, which at last became united and arranged in such ways as to produce our Universe. But it would be easier to believe that St. Paul's Cathedral was reared by the mere dumping down of a sufficient number of loads of stones, which were then left to find their own places in the structure. Apart from any question as to how the original fire-mist came into being, there are traces everywhere in the Universe of the work of *a guiding Mind, the Architect of the great Building*.

If you pick up a book at random, and find, first, words that you can understand, then sentences that you can understand, and then a sustained argument that you can understand, you feel justified in saying that it is the work of some one with a mind like your own, even though there may be parts of it beyond your comprehension. For the scientist, Nature is such a book ; he finds one chapter in the stars, and another in the rocks, and another in the plants ; and, though there are paragraphs in each chapter that he does not yet comprehend, he finds the book as a whole clear and intelligible. Moreover, he finds that what he reads in one chapter agrees with what he learns in another ; that he can trace in Geology the same kind of law, method, and order that he finds in Astronomy, Chemistry or Botany ; and that all scientific knowledge combines to form a consistent whole. The Book of Nature gives us a sustained, consistent argument, and there must have been *a Mind to produce that Book*.

Hence we feel justified in saying that *the Universe is the creation of a Mind that works on similar lines to our own*.

The Theory of Evolution. At first sight it may appear as if the argument just stated cannot hold good in face of the modern *Theory of Evolution*.

It should be noted, however, that belief in a Creator does not tie us down to any one view of His *method* in His creating work. Until comparatively recently it was generally supposed that the various species of plants and animals were made by a separate creative act in each case. But the modern Theory of Evolution, asserts that Life began in some exceedingly simple form, such as a little bit of jelly-like protoplasm, and that in the course of ages higher forms of life developed from the lower by successive minute improvements. Let us suppose that in any given species an animal was born, by chance, with some peculiar feature that gave it an advantage over its companions in the struggle for food, or some new kind of protection against its foes. Obviously it would have a greater chance of surviving. If its offspring inherited this peculiar feature too, as they multiplied the privileged variety would win the whole field, and the ordinary variety would die out. For instance, as bears moved towards the Arctic regions, those born with the thickest fur would have greater protection against the cold, and those born with the lightest-coloured fur would have the advantage of being less conspicuous to their enemies, and to their prey ; and so, by degrees, the Polar Bear, with its thick white fur, would come into existence as a new variety, and become the only variety in those regions.

Further, the theory accounts, not only for the development of higher species, but also for the increase in the number of species. Thus, the original cat living in the jungle eventually became the striped tiger, since its coat of yellow striped with black would make it almost invisible there, where everything is seen in small patches of bright sunlight alternating with bars of dark shadow. On the other hand, the same animal living in the sandy deserts became the tawny lion, whose colour makes it almost invisible against the sand. In this way it appears quite conceivable that the many species of animals we know may all have sprung originally from some very much lower and simpler form of life.

When first mooted, it was thought that this theory sufficed to explain the Universe, without the work of a creating God. But:

(1) It has not, at present, explained how *life* itself began.

(2) It has not yet bridged over certain great gaps in the chain of development: e.g., the beginning of *consciousness*, which distinguishes the higher forms of animal from vegetable life ; and the beginning of *self-conscious reason*, which distinguishes Man from the brutes.

(3) It only supposes *another method* in God's creating work, a gradual process instead of a few distinct acts of creation at the beginning.

Evolution does not enable us to dispense with God ; and it may, indeed, be claimed that the conception of God as creating through all the ages is nobler than the old view, and that it perhaps finds confirmation in the words of Jesus, " My Father worketh even until now " (John v. 17). It should be noted that the successive " days," or periods, in the Creation Story (Gen. i.) agree in their general order with the scheme of Evolution. Most Christian students, however, stipulate for the direct action of the creating God at such critical points as those named above.

On this view Man would come into being by development through a long line of animal ancestors as regards his body, but by a distinct act of God as concerns the higher nature, or " soul," that constitutes him a human being.

But, though these striking gaps in the chain of development exist and are never likely to be filled up, our belief in God as Creator does not depend upon them. The work of God is as necessary in the infinitesimally small steps of progress as in the greater ones'; and, even if we could be shown an absolutely unbroken chain of development from non-living matter up to Man, we should still be unable to dispense with the idea of a creating God.

The answer to the question *How?* is, therefore:

By the creating work of an Intelligent God, working probably by gradual Evolution to produce higher types of life, and, almost certainly, with direct creative action at certain critical points.

3. *Indications of purpose.* The third question is, *Why has the World come into existence?* We find that in countless ways animal and vegetable life on the Earth are suited to and fitted for the World to which they belong. Our lungs are adapted for breathing in the atmosphere, and the gills of the fish for breathing in water. Our legs are adapted for movement upon the ground, and the bird's wings for movement in the air. Some plants are adapted to tropical heat, others to Arctic cold.

As we have seen above, some of these adaptations may have come about by Evolution. But what made the Evolution possible? Is not the answer, that the development of his thick white fur became possible to the Polar Bear, because God wished to have creatures capable of comfortable life among the eternal snows? and that the development of wings became possible to the bird, because God wished to have creatures capable of joyous flight in the air? However much the bear might feel the need of a thicker coat and a whiter one in such surroundings, he *could not* have produced it by mere desire or effort of his own. It was *the will of God* that made the Evolution possible. And, even if it be supposed that the ancestor of the giraffe may have lengthened its neck by straining to reach the leaves of trees, it could not have passed on that longer neck to its offspring, for only *inborn* characteristics can be transmitted by heredity.

Now the World is adapted in an extraordinary number

of ways to give *Man* a comfortable existence, rich in the pleasures of sight, sound, taste, smell, and feeling. Is it not reasonable to say that in all the stages through which the World passed in the making, and through which Man passed in the making, God had *a great purpose* in view : *to make a World in which Man could dwell, and then to make Man to dwell in it?*

But it may be urged that, even if this explains the existence of the Earth, it does not account for the larger Universe ; and that the Earth is so small, and Man so insignificant, that it is incredible that the heavenly bodies were made only to shine as stars in his sky. To this we reply, How do we know that intelligent life is confined to the Earth? Other worlds may be inhabited. And if it seems hard in that case to believe that God could have selected this little planet to be the scene of the Incarnation, this may, for all we know, be the one fallen world, the one lost sheep of God's flock. Those who hold the Christian faith are quite free to admit that there may be other worlds ; and can feel sure that, whatever their needs of Revelation and Redemption may be, God has not failed to meet them.

The answer to the question *Why?* is, therefore, that:

The World appears to have been made, in fulfilment of God's purpose, to be the home of Life, and especially of Man.

C.—CONSCIENCE IN MAN

Turning from the World around us to look within, we find a further reason for our belief in God. For we become aware of a strange feeling of responsibility to an Authority beyond ourselves, and greater than Society. Men who have broken no law of the State often feel that they have offended against a *higher law*. Again and again those who have escaped detection in crime, and who have nothing to fear from the officers of justice, have felt themselves compelled by an *inner voice* to make confession of their deed.

It is hardly right, perhaps, to call Conscience " the voice of God," for a corrupted and perverted conscience may err in its judgment, so that a man may be a persecutor, like Saul of Tarsus, in obedience to his Conscience. But, though a man may err in his judgment as to what is right or wrong, Conscience never errs in its insistence that:

(1) There is *a real difference* between Right and Wrong ; and that,

(2) We *must* do what we believe to be the Right, whether we like it or not.

We saw at the beginning that Man naturally and instinctively believes in a God of some kind. *Conscience means that Man naturally and instinctively recognizes that God as his Moral Ruler.*

It is very significant, too, that we cannot frame an entirely satisfactory definition of Right, or a really convincing reason why we ought to do the Right, that does not involve belief in God.

CONCLUSION

To sum up, we believe in God:

1. *Because the belief is so universal and persistent as to be almost an instinct.*

2. *Because we find in the World*

   (1) *A Creator,* (2) *An Intelligent Creator,* (3) *A Creator with a Purpose.*

3. *Because our consciences declare that there is a Moral Ruler.*

Yet, although the evidences seem so clear, the distressing fact remains that many do not believe in God, or, at least, have no clear personal conviction of His existence ; and the question presses, *Why do not all believe?*

To begin with, it should be noted that there is a wide difference between a reasoned creed and the experience of God as a precious reality. Such arguments as have been set forth above do not, by themselves, yield more than an abstract belief in God, similar to our belief in the North Pole. A living faith in God involves the heart and the will as well as the intellect.

In the case of the average Christian man, belief is in part the result of tradition and upbringing, coupled with

[torn fragment overlaying page:]

WHAT A CHRISTIAN BELIEVES

15—20. We have no reason to be surprised, how-
if there should prove to be some discrepancies, that
may find it impossible to reconcile in our present
...fect state of being. Is it not a common experience
...ear that a friend has done something that seems quite
...sistent with a letter he wrote to us, or a conversat...
...he had with us, on the same subject? Yet wh...
...t him he can so explain matters, that his action
...erstood becomes quite consistent with...
...perly understood. Our present dis...
...ause our under...

[upper right, partially obscured:]

of God. Then comes
...xistence of God is not
very highly probable.
..., by which the man says,
...act as if the belief were
...e finds it true in experience,
...y works.

...not take this step?

...feared, are hindered by their
...consequences, and to live the
...belief in God should involve (see

...some who are not held back by any such considerations, and whose lives are blameless, are prevented from
finding God by some unfortunate experience, which has
warped their spiritual vision or prejudiced them against
Religion.

(3) The case of some of the very noblest of mankind,
who long to find God and yet seek Him in vain, may conceivably be accounted for by supposing that, just as some
poor children are born physically blind, some may possibly
be born spiritually blind. If so, we may regard such men
as God's blind children ; and we may be sure that, as the
blind child is specially dear to the earthly father, so God's
blind children receive a special measure of His love, even
though they cannot look into His face.

CHAPTER II

OUR KNOWLEDGE OF GOD AND ITS SOURCES

A.—CAN WE KNOW GOD?

It being clear that we have the right to believe in God,
the question arises, Can we know Him?

Beginning with T. H. Huxley, a considerable body of
scientists and philosophers have contended that, though
there is a God, it is impossible for us to know Him. They
call themselves *Agnostics,* a name derived from the inscrip-

tion: AGNOSTO THEO ("To an *u...*
St. Paul found on the altar at Athe...
Or perhaps Huxley wished to contrast hi...
early Christian heretical sects the "Gnostics,"...
a special kind of knowledge (*gnosis*), and so calle...
an *a*gnostic, the *a*- being the Greek prefix meaning "...

But before we allow that God is unknowable, we have
a right to ask what it is that constitutes this impossibility.
God's infinite Nature, His Absoluteness, His Spirituality,
says the Agnostic. But if we know that He is infinite,
absolute and spiritual, we already know three great facts
about Him, so that He cannot be altogether unknowable.

The Christian makes no claim to know God *fully or
exhaustively*. We cannot know even the commonest
objects of nature fully or exhaustively: they all suggest
questions that we cannot answer.

> Flower in the crannied wall,
> I pluck you out of the crannies,
> I hold you here, root and all, in my hand,
> Little flower—but *if* I could understand
> What you are, root and all, and all in all,
> I should know what God and man is.
> —*Tennyson*.

So the Bible proclaims of God that "His greatness is
unsearchable," and that we only "know in part," Or,
as the hymn puts it,

> Beneath Thy feet we lie afar,
> And see but shadows of Thy face.

Yet we claim that the little we do know is *true* knowledge
so far as it goes. We are a long way from having an
exhaustive knowledge of the Sun. Yet a single ray of
light from the Sun, passing through a spectroscope, suffices
to show us with absolute certainty that the Sun consists
of precisely the same chemical elements as our own Earth.
Our present knowledge of God is not all that we shall know
of Him in the future ; and it is expressed in words and
metaphors belonging to our earthly life, since we have
no other words to describe the unseen and the spiritual ;
but it suffices to guide, to inspire, and to gladden us.

or in pri...

4. Personal intercou...

Similar ways of knowing God are open to us.

We follow the first method when we study the works of God in *Nature* and in *History,* and what they teach us is known as *Natural Religion.* We follow the second and third methods in our study of the *Bible,* for it claims to be the record of (1) what good men thought and felt about God over many centuries, and (2) of words spoken by God to men through His messengers. The teaching of the Bible is called *Revealed or Supernatural Religion,* because it is believed to have come to us in supernatural ways. The Christian also claims that He can follow the fourth method, and commune with God in personal intercourse, cf. " That they should *know* Thee, the only true God " (John xvii. 3). What we learn of God in this way is the teaching of *Personal Religion.* This will be treated incidentally in later chapters. At this point we have to consider the other sources, namely, our knowledge of God through Nature, History, and the Bible.

The question at once arises, *Can these different kinds of knowledge disagree?* The revelations of God through Nature and through Scripture are beautifully compared and contrasted in Psalm xix. It is obvious that if they are both true revelations of God, they must agree: there can be no final contradiction between what Science *proves* to be true and the *real* teaching of the Bible, if the Bible is a genuine revelation of God. There have been many *apparent* contradictions, arising either from unproved scientific theories, afterwards discarded, or from misunderstanding of the teaching of the Bible. There are also differences which may be accounted for in ways suggested

difficulties often arise
understanding of Nature is far from complete
our interpretation of the Bible is far from perfect ;
and, at the best, Nature and the Bible together only show
us *part* of the mind of God. Some of these apparent contradictions, such as that between God's Sovereignty and
Man's Free Will, may never be reconciled here ; but, just
in proportion as we reach truer Science and truer Bible
interpretation, the difficulties will diminish in number.

Meanwhile we are bound to accept whatever Science
definitely and finally *proves*. If it appears to conflict
with the Bible, we must look for fuller light on the teaching of the Bible ; and if reconciliation still seems hopeless,
we must be content to wait for the fuller knowledge that
will come with the larger life beyond, when we shall no
longer " know in part."

We can pass now to a more detailed consideration of
these sources of our knowledge of God.

1. *The Message of Nature*

(1) *Nature's message to the Scientist*. In all ages and
all lands men have been impressed by certain great
features of the natural world, which reveal to us various
aspects of the Creator. With all improvements in our
apparatus, this teaching becomes only more impressive.
The Agnostic may claim that God is personally unknowable, but he does not deny what Nature suggests.

Not only for the Psalmist, but for all men, " The
heavens declare the glory of God." Sweeping them with
the *telescope*, we are bewildered with the immeasurable
distances, the vastness of the spheres, and the stupendous

movements, and we are almost
... the *Power and Majesty* of the Creator.
the study of life in its minutest forms through
the ...roscope, we find endless indications of infinite care
and skill shown in the structure of creatures almost inconceivably small, and so we are led to believe in the *Universal
Presence and Activity* of God.

The student of Chemistry, Physics, or Biology working
in his *laboratory* finds in his turn a world of order and
method, working according to laws so fixed and reliable
that the results can be exactly calculated. We are bound
to believe in *the Wisdom, the Sovereignty, and the Unchangeableness of God*.

(2) *Nature's message to the Artist.* The work of
Nature is almost always either beautiful or majestic. Man
may mar a landscape with a railway cutting or embank-
ment, but Nature sets to work at once to restore its beauty
with herbage and with foliage. Some creatures strike us
as ugly, but the most hideous apes and the vilest of slugs
show a beautiful perfection of finish in the structure of
their parts. Some forms of beauty may be explained as
mere devices to secure the propagation of life, as, for
instance, the beauty and the scent of flowers, designed to
attract the bees and so secure the fertilization of the plants.
But that does not explain the beauty of most landscapes
or the beautiful forms of the clouds: their beauty is not
necessary for any merely useful purpose. And so we are
led to believe in the God of *Beauty*.

(3) *Nature's message to the Christian.* It is obvious
that what will be suggested to a man by observation
depends largely on what is already in his mind. One who
is familiar with the Law of Gravitation will detect its working, not only in the falling of an apple, but also in the
ebb and flow of the tides and the movements of the
heavenly bodies. In the same way the Christian man,
familiar with the teaching of the Bible, finds in Nature,
not only such truths as those mentioned above, but also
confirmation of others. The telescope leads him to believe
that "*with God nothing is impossible.*" The microscope
confirms his faith in a *Providence* that watches over all.

The unchangeable laws discovere
to him of the *Faithfulness* of God in in
the beauty of the landscape further suggest
the God who creates beauty must Himself be
Holy ; and that, if He creates it for Man's delight, He
must be *Loving.*

2. *The Message of History*

What we know of the life of men, and especially the
history of the nations studied in its larger aspects, has
much to teach us concerning God.

(1) *A God of Purpose.* In the case of probably every
nation that has risen to eminence, we can detect some need
of men that it satisfied, or some purpose that it served
in the progress of the race. The little states of Greece
have taught the world Art and Philosophy. The city of
Rome became a mighty empire, and, in spite of its decay,
it has taught the whole modern world the principles of
Law and Government. The little people of the Hebrews
rose out of obscurity to greatness: they are now a homeless, wandering folk ; but they have taught the Western
world Religion. Is it unreasonable to believe, in view
of these facts, that there is "a God that ruleth in the
affairs of men," *a God with a Purpose?*

(2) *A God of Righteousness.* The most sceptical
students of History are ready to admit that there is
"something that looks very like a Nemesis" pursuing the
wrongdoer. As Matthew Arnold put it, we can discern
"A Power not ourselves that makes for righteousness."
Behind the decay of great and wealthy empires there has
always been national sin and the slackening of moral fibre.
"The mills of God" do, indeed, "grind slowly, but they
grind exceeding small." History points to *a God of
Righteousness and of Judgment.*

3. *The Message of the Bible*

At the heart of the Christian Religion lies the belief
that God has spoken to men "by the prophets" and "in

His Son," and that this revelation has come down to us in the Bible.

No book has ever been, or now is, so widely circulated ; no book has been so minutely and lovingly studied ; and no book in the literature of the world can compare with it in influence. Yet no book has been so fiercely attacked by foes, nor has any book suffered so much from the misunderstanding and mistaken zeal of its friends.

(1) *Some Preliminary Considerations*

A large part of the perplexity that is commonly felt to-day about the Bible would never have arisen if certain facts were generally understood and allowed for in our reading of the Bible.

(*a*) *The Bible is not a book, but a library,* the work of many writers covering a period of 1500 years. They were men differing as much in their surroundings, their interests, their habits of thought, and their general outlook, as our early Saxon writers, and Chaucer, Shakespeare, Bunyan, Tennyson and Westcott. We can do justice to their writings only by allowing for such differences ; and we have no right to be surprised if we find occasional discrepancies, either in their ways of stating a fact, or in their moral and religious teaching.

(*b*) *The Bible employs all the forms of literature :* History, Biography, Philosophy, Sermon, Drama, Poetry, Song, Hymn, Prayer, Parable, Fable, and Old-world Story. Obviously this must be allowed for, and we must not interpret an ironical passage as sober statement of fact, or a delicate poetic fancy as literal prose. If we bear in mind that the precious thing in the Bible is its revelation of religious truth, it will not greatly trouble us if we find that scholars describe the Story of Creation or the Story of the Fall as old-world legends. So long as the cup is clean and the water is pure, the thirsty man will not complain because he is asked to drink from a quaint child's cup. Why should it trouble us if the Water of Life comes to us sometimes in a quaint cup of the world's childhood, a picturesque old-world legend? The cup is certainly clean, for these two stories at the opening of Genesis differ from corresponding stories in other nations by their freedom from the taint of heathenism. And the water in the cup is good, for the stories contain great and precious and eternal truths concerning God, Man, and Sin. It is the water, and not the cup, that is the important thing to the thirsty man.

(c) *The Bible is a revelation of Religion, not intended to be a textbook of Science,* or of other subjects which men can investigate by natural means ; since God does not do for men that which they can do for themselves, or reveal to them that which they can discover for themselves. The Science of the Bible is not the Science of the 20th century: in these things the Bible reflects the ideas of Nature current at the time, and uses the only language that the people of the time could understand. In the same way, if inaccuracies should be detected in details of the History, they need not weaken our confidence in the moral and religious teaching of the Bible. It should be noted, however, that the general accuracy of the Bible is finding remarkable confirmation in research among the monuments of Assyria in the case of the Old Testament, and the rubbish heaps of Asia Minor and Ancient Egypt in the case of the New.

(d) *Some books of the Bible are of complicated authorship.* The writers of such books as Kings or Chronicles refer to existing records, which they used in the compilation of their histories ; and St. Luke does the same in the case of his Gospel. *The Higher Criticism* is the attempt to separate matter derived from different sources. For many years scholars have been examining the Bible with this aim, and especially the books of the Old Testament ; and it is claimed that several books which were formerly thought to be the work of single authors show signs of such compilation. Some of the most notable conclusions are:

(i) That in the Pentateuch we have writings coming down from the time of Moses, but several times edited and enlarged before they reached their present form.

(ii) That the poets who gave us the Psalms were far more numerous than was formerly supposed, and that many of the Psalms were not composed until after the Exile.

(iii) That the Book of Isaiah consists of at least two main parts, chapters i.- xxxix. and chapters xl.- lxvi., the first the work of the prophet Isaiah, who lived before the Exile, the second the work of an unknown prophet during the Exile. The two books were bound up together, possibly because the second prophet may have borne the same name ; but more probably because he was regarded as continuing the work of his great predecessor.

The process of division and analysis has been carried a long way, and the conclusions of the more extreme critics are almost absurdly fantastic and contradictory. A few of the broadest conclusions, such as those mentioned above, are, however, accepted by the great majority of Christian students. If they finally prove to be true, they need not imperil the authority of the Bible: they would only indicate that God gave us His revelation more gradually, and by a larger number of inspired writers, than was formerly supposed.

Some of the more extreme Criticism is, on the contrary, a menace to the Christian faith. It not only carries the analysis to absurd lengths, but ignores, and virtually denies, the claim of the religion of the Bible to be in any special sense a direct revelation from God. The methods used are often quite capricious and unfair. In many cases the tests employed are what is called " subjective." That is to say, a critic will alter or discard a passage, not for any reason that he can justify to others, but merely because he *thinks* or *feels* that it is out of place. Thus the Bible is mutilated to agree with critical theories, when the fair thing would obviously be to modify the critical theories to square with the facts of the Bible. The Bible has emerged triumphant from such attacks before, and will do so again.

(e) *The Bible is progressive in its teaching about Religion and Morals*. The earliest parts belong to the childhood of the race: the religious ideas of Abraham, for instance, are as simple as those of a little child. But the Bible records *a revelation that became fuller* as time went on. Thus, each of the Prophets had some favourite thought about God: Isaiah, His *holiness;* Amos, His *judgment;* Hosea, His *mercy.* Line by line the picture is filled in, until in the New Testament we are shown the God of Love, the God and Father of our Lord Jesus Christ. It has been objected that a perfect God would have given a perfect revelation in the first instance. But is it not more in keeping with perfect wisdom that the revelation should have been gradual, coming to men in successive stages, as they were able to grasp it and to profit by it?

In the same way *the moral standard* in the Bible gradually rises. There are deeds recorded in the earlier history of the nation, and wishes expressed in certain of the Psalms, that appear to us immoral and barbarous. We are bound to admit this, though it should be noted that at its lowest the morality of Israel was always higher than that of surrounding nations. But the fact that there is much in the Old Testament of which the Christian conscience disapproves, only indicates that it was step by step that men moved upward to reach the heights of the Sermon on the Mount and St. Paul's great chapter on Love.

It follows from this that *the New Testament supersedes the Old, both in Theology and in Morals;* and that, whenever the two appear to clash, we must accept the verdict of the New Testament.

It may be asked, What then is the use of the Old Testament?

(i) The fascinating stories which tell of God's dealings with the nation and with individuals, and the records of men's sins and failures, and of their aspirations and strivings after goodness, will always remain of measureless practical worth.

(ii) There is a wealth of material in such books as Job, the Psalms and the Prophets, which is not reproduced in the New Testament.

(iii) We need the Old Testament that we may fully understand the New. A man has not mastered a business until he has worked his way up from the bottom ; and we cannot fully understand the New Testament conception of God and of life, until we have followed the path by which men climbed to reach " the truth as it is in Jesu."

(*f*) It is quite impossible to hope ever to obtain the original autograph of any book of the Bible. The best and oldest Manuscripts we have are *the result of several copyings,* and we all know the difficulty of copying without mistakes. We can distinguish *several kinds of error :*

(i) Words are sometimes mis-spelt, or omitted, or inserted, through the carelessness of the copyist.

(ii) There are a few cases in which a marginal note has been inserted as part of the text in the new copy. As the R.V. indicates, John vii. 53 - viii. 11 is a passage of this kind. It is almost certainly a true story of Jesus, but was certainly not included in the Gospel as first written.

(iii) There are a very few cases in which the text has been altered to make it agree with some opinion of the copyist. The reference to the three heavenly Witnesses in 1 John v. 7 (A.V.) is an instance. The copyist was probably deeply interested in the doctrine of the Trinity, and the threefold earthly witness, described in verse 8, suggested to him a threefold heavenly witness.

By *Textual Criticism,* that is, the most minute comparison of hundreds of copies, scholars have been able to arrive at a text of the New Testament which must be almost exactly what the authors wrote. In the case of the Old Testament the difficulties are greater: our copies are all late, the language is harder, and trifling changes in the vowel-points may entirely alter the meaning of a word. The result is that there are a number of doubtful passages, and a few that are quite unintelligible as the text stands.

Some of our difficulties would disappear with a purer text. But at the same time, the number of doubtful passages is comparatively small, and there is no doctrine which depends for its support on a disputed reading. The substantial accuracy of our copies, after they have passed through so many hands, is almost a miracle: nothing like it is found in the case of any other ancient book.

But the fact that our Bible is a translation makes it of the utmost importance that we should use the most accurate possible version, and the one based upon the most accurate possible text. The more we believe in the Divine authority of the Bible, the more imperative it is to use such modern translations as the Revised Version, Moffatt's *New Translation* (Old and New Testaments), The *Twentieth Century New Testament*, and Weymouth's *New Testament in Modern Speech*.

(2) *The Unique Authority of the Bible*

Enough has been said to make it clear that minor errors and discrepancies of various kinds may exist in the Bible, without destroying its claim to be *a Unique Revelation and Guide to Truth*. We may now consider this claim.

(*a*) For the Christian it is a fact of great importance that *Jesus used the Old Testament*. It seems clear that as a boy He must have learnt Hebrew in order to read it, for His mother-tongue was Aramaic. He continually quoted it, both to illustrate and to confirm His teaching ; and He quoted from very nearly every book. Scripture was His weapon in temptation, and He died with words of Scripture on His lips. Clearly a book that held such a place in the life of Jesus must have very special claims upon His followers.

(*b*) *We may compare the Bible with other sacred books*. It is only just to admit that there are beautiful sayings in some of the sacred books of other faiths. But the number of them is very small, and there is no comparison between these books and the Bible in general tone and in moral and spiritual elevation. This can easily be tested by the reading of a few pages of the Koran. The Bible often records moral lapses on the part of its heroes, but it never condones them ; and, as was stated above, when the moral standard of Israel was lowest, it was still far higher than that of surrounding nations. There is also a directness, simplicity and intelligibility in the Bible teaching concerning God, that are not to be found elsewhere. In other books either the gods are depicted as cruel and immoral, or we are hopelessly bewildered in the attempt to distinguish between a multitude of semi-divine beings, who are described in almost unintelligible language.

(c) In all these centuries *men have not improved upon the Bible :* neither poets, nor preachers, nor saints have added to what we may find there. Henry Rogers, in an essay entitled *The Blank Bible,* pictured a day when every copy of the Bible was destroyed, and every idea borrowed directly or indirectly from the Bible blotted out of English literature. How much would be left to guide, comfort, or encourage us? Almost nothing!

(d) There is *a wonderful unity and consistency* about the Bible. Say, if you will, that small discrepancies exist, and that the later teaching sometimes supersedes and annuls the earlier ; yet:

(i) The Bible never falters in its witness to God and to Righteousness.

(ii) There is a single purpose to reveal God with increasing fulness.

(iii) The Old Testament leads up to the New, and the New completes the Old. The Mosaic sacrifices all led up to the Sacrifice on Calvary, the Prophets found their fulfilment in the Life and Death of Christ, and the spiritual longings expressed in the Psalms are satisfied by the Work of Christ and of the Holy Spirit.

Yet the Bible was written by a multitude of writers, in many different ages, with no combined plan, unless that plan existed in the mind of God.

(e) *Miracles.* The Bible narratives declare that those who claimed to be God's messengers were in several cases endowed with miraculous power, by which their message was confirmed to their hearers. Such evidence would, of course, be conclusive to those who saw the miracles ; but it cannot have much weight with us, until we find reasons for believing that the miracles really happened. But there is only one, the Resurrection of Jesus, for which we have any evidence beyond the Bible statement. Can we satisfy ourselves that they actually happened?

(i) As is shown on pp. 49—51, there is ample evidence that the Resurrection of Jesus was a real historical fact.

(ii) This being so, other miracles become possible and, indeed, probable.

(iii) In both the Old and the New Testaments the miracles are described in a perfectly sober, matter-of-fact way. They fit naturally into the narrative, and they generally "sound possible." A great revelation of God would be a fitting occasion for miracles, and most of them impress us as worthy of the occasion.

In fact, if miracles are possible at all, and the Resurrection proves that they are, there is little reason to deny most of the others. It is, perhaps, not impossible that one or two legendary stories may have crept in amongst the miracles of Elisha ; and it is almost certain that in one or two cases, as, for instance, in the story of Joshua and the Sun, the average reader sees a miracle where a more accurate interpretation would show that none is implied. In the same way, it is rather doubtful whether any miracle is represented in the story of the Coin in the mouth of the Fish. Most such cases are dealt with in detail in the commentaries.

But apart from difficulties connected with a few of the incidents, we have a good right to believe in the miracles as a whole, and to see in them a proof that those who wrought them were messengers of God.

(f) *Prophecy.* The Bible asserts of each of a number of notable men that "the word of the Lord came unto him." It is a common impression that the Prophets were chiefly concerned to foretell the future. They did this to some extent, and the Bible records instances in which their predictions were realized ; but their main work was certainly to *tell forth,* or preach. Yet there is one great prediction running through the Old Testament, the fulfilment of which no one can dispute: the promise of the Coming of Christ. "The testimony of Jesus is the spirit of prophecy" (Rev. xix. 10), that is, the essence of prophecy is found in its witness to Christ. It begins as early as the Fall (Gen. iii. 15) ; we can trace it in the words of Moses (Deut. xviii. 15) ; it occurs in extraordinary detail in certain of the Psalms (e.g., Ps. lxxii.) ; and right through the Prophets we find the hope growing in its clearness and fulness, until it became possible to write such a passage as Isa. liii.

It may be that in some instances the Prophet hardly knew how much he was foretelling, and himself expected some smaller and speedier fulfilment. But the extraordinary fact remains that a large number of men, writing over a long period and with no combined plan, writing, as they thought, about small and local affairs, yet wrote what found complete and exact fulfilment centuries afterwards in Jesus Christ. The prophecy of Christ is *a miracle of literature,* that nothing can ever rob of its wonder: a miracle that can neither be denied nor explained away.

(3) *The Inspiration of the Bible*

Most of the difficulties of this subject arise from the attempt to define too exactly either the meaning or the method of Inspiration. There are few readers of the Bible who do not recognize in it a strange spiritual quality ; but it is no easy thing to describe it, or to form a theory of it.

It is safest to use the words of the Bible itself, and to say, " Men spake from God, being moved by the Holy Ghost " (2 Peter i. 21). The theory of Verbal Inspiration regards the Bible as virtually dictated word for word by God. But such a theory goes beyond what the facts we know concerning the history of the books will permit, and beyond any claim that the Bible makes for itself.

The word *inspiration* means an in-breathing, and suggests that the Spirit of God was breathed into the sacred writers, and so " moved " or stimulated their minds that they were able to grasp and to express the great revelation.

The *purpose* of Inspiration was clearly to give us knowledge of God that we could not have obtained without Divine assistance ; and this we find abundantly in the Bible.

As to its *extent,* the writers of the Bible were inspired just in so far as they fulfil this purpose, and give us such knowledge of God. The Inspiration would presumably begin where the natural human powers failed ; and the degree of Inspiration would thus vary with the degree of supernatural aid needed to write what was written. Heb. i. 1 tells us that God spoke by the prophets " by *divers* portions and in *divers* manners.'' Divine aid would not be needed for details of fact, such as those of history, science, or geography: the responsibility for these rests on the writer, the Spirit being responsible only for the teaching about God. On this view, the degree of Inspiration in the Epistle to the Romans would be very high, that in the Book of Esther very low. The case of the Historical Books of the Old Testament, to take one example, might be described thus:

(i) There is a measure of Inspiration in the fact that the writers were describing the history of what may be called an *inspired race,* a chosen people, the whole course of whose fortunes was meant to teach the world about God.

(ii) Further Inspiration would be needed to discern the moral and spiritual teaching of the history, and so to tell the story as to make this clear.

(iii) For the mere historical facts the writers would have to use, and did actually use, the official records kept at the Court and such other sources of information as were open to them. The accuracy of the Books of Kings or Chronicles in such matters thus depends on the accuracy of the contemporary records.

In the case of the Gospels, however, the Saviour's promise in John xiv. 26 gives us the right to believe that the disciples were specially assisted by the Spirit to recall His words and deeds with accuracy.

(4) *The Value of the Bible*

Here again we must be careful not to claim more than the Bible claims for itself. It is described as '' a lamp unto (our) feet, and a light unto (our) path '' (Ps. cxix. 105); and it is compared to '' a lamp shining in a dark place '' (2 Peter i. 19). The picture is that of a man crossing a dark moor by the light of a lantern. Now a *lantern* is not the *sun,* lighting up the whole scene and making all things clear. So, too, the Bible does not give us all the knowledge of God that we shall have in the life to come, and does not illumine all the darkness here: there are many things we should like to know that it does not tell us.

But the lantern does make the path clear and cast a little circle of light around; and that suffices for the traveller to find his way. So, too, the Bible gives us *light sufficient* to see the path of duty and to find our way Home.

And what is the value of such a lantern to the man lost in the darkness? It is *priceless,* it is worth any sum that he can give. So we may say of the Scriptures, " More to be desired are they than gold, yea, than much fine gold " (Ps. xix. 10).

(5) *Another way of approaching the Bible*

There is another method of approaching the question of the Bible that is simpler, and in some ways more satisfactory.

How did the early converts among the Gentiles approach the Bible? They were convinced by preaching, and won by what they heard of Christ. Then they learnt of the Old Testament as the Book that led up to Christ, and the Book which the Saviour Himself used on earth. As, from time to time, any books of the New Testament appeared, they would become sacred to them as telling the story of Christ's life, or carrying forward and expanding His teaching.

The same method is open to us. Most men are won to Christ and come under His spell by hearing the Gospel preached, or by reading the Gospel records, *without any theory of Inspiration* in their minds. It is an easy thing then to use the Old Testament *because* Jesus used it, and *as* Jesus used it, and to give it the place of honour that He gave to it. As for the New Testament, that will become to such a man the Book of Books, with its record of the Saviour's life and words, and the further teaching of His chosen band.

The advantage of this method is twofold:

(i) It saves us from attempting to define the sacred mystery of Inspiration too strictly.

(ii) It builds our faith on Christ Himself, and not upon a book, even though that book be the Bible. Many attacks may threaten the Bible, and even a sneer about Jonah and the whale may disturb the minds of some, if their whole trust is in the Bible. But the man whose faith rests directly on the Personal Christ is "built on a Rock that cannot move."

Some have to say that they believe in Christ because they believe in the Bible ; those are happier who can say that they believe in the Bible because they believe in Christ.

CHAPTER III

WHAT WE BELIEVE ABOUT GOD

WE are now in a position to regard the Bible as an authority in all matters of Religion and Morals. In attempting to define and arrange in order what are known as the Attributes, or Characteristics, of God, we may divide them into two groups:

1. Those which men have discovered without the Bible, though they are also taught in the Bible.
2. Those which we should not know apart from the Bible.

A.—ATTRIBUTES OF GOD DISCOVERED BY REASON AND CONFIRMED IN THE BIBLE

1. *There is only one God*. Nothing is more certain to the modern mind than that, if God exists, He must be One. The heathen conception of many gods, with limited powers and rival interests, cannot possibly survive when once the modern idea of the Universe is grasped. For, if Science proves anything, it is that the Universe is a real *unity*, the work of one Creating Power, which governs and directs the whole.

Though it was centuries before the mass of the nation of Israel sincerely believed it, the most important part of God's early revelation of Himself to them was expressed in the words, "Hear, O Israel: the Lord our God is *one* Lord " (Deut. vi. 4).

This belief neither affirms nor denies the existence of spiritual beings intermediate between God and Man, such as the Angels and Archangels of the Bible. Indeed, one of the greatest of modern scientists, the late Dr. Alfred Russel Wallace, the co-discoverer with Darwin of Evolu-

tion, earnestly believed in the existence of successive grades of beings higher than Man, through whom God executes His will, and through whom He ministers to and cares for Man. Cf. with this, Heb. i. 14.

2. *God is a Spirit.* What we mean by Spirit is best understood by contrast with what we call Matter. All th can be seen, heard, smelt, tasted, handled, measured weighed, and all that can give us the feeling of hea cold, hardness or softness, and the like, is Matter. bodies are material, because they have a particula size, weight and colour. But we are distinctly that our real Self is something within, that can seen nor touched, and this we call Mind or S

It is the teaching both of Reason and of th " God is a Spirit " (John iv. 24). The believing it are that:

(1) One who is Lord of the Universe ca be cramped and limited by material co we are subject to in our bodies.

(2) Mind or Spirit is a higher for Matter, and the Supreme Being m form of existence. Mind can meas Matter ; it can alter its forms, stances ; it can control and us making pen, ink, and paper i thought to others. It is even a apart from Mind to receive a which Matter gives rise, ther That, however, is too prof tary book, and belongs to

If we are right in belie that idolatry is both God cannot be wor image (cf. Isa. xliv. always the degrada ception of God. ruption (see Rom

If God is a S Him " in spiri

3. *God is a Person.* We mean by a Person, not necessarily a being dwelling in a body, but any centre of Love, Thought and Will, that can distinguish itself from the rest of the Universe, and is conscious of being a distinct Individual. Clearly, if God is not a Person, there can be no real truth in Christianity, for in that case there can be neither love nor communion between Him and Man. Our reasons for believing in the Personality of God are:

(1) That we ourselves are persons. There is nothing of which each of us is so certain as that "I am I," something quite distinct from all other persons or things. But it cannot be that God has made creatures greater and more wonderful than Himself ; and, if we are persons, He must possess a personality at least as complete as ours.

(2) All the traces that we find of Purpose and of the work of Intelligence in Nature favour the belief in God's personality.

(3) The Bible throughout speaks of God as a Person, feelings and affections corresponding to our own.

Pantheism

leading system of thought which denies the Personality of God is called *Pantheism,* from the Greek words and *God.* It teaches that All is God and God is or that God is merely the Soul of which the visible is the Garment ; so that the Universe, good and bad alike, is God, and God has no independent

consequences, if this be true, are fatal to

makes it impossible to believe either in the Fatherhood, or in a Personal Providence, or in Prayer. makes God the author of Sin, for the evil is all equally with the good. It thus undermines sin and of moral responsibility. Indeed, in the word *sin* is almost meaningless.

away all belief in Personal Immortality: soul is part of God, and, at death, is returned, and lost, as the river is lost in the ocean. errors, however, Pantheism includes an

element of truth. Christianity teaches what is known as *the Immanence of God,* that is, that God is present every-where and in everything, however lowly. Note such a text as, " In Him we live, and move, and have our being " (Acts xvii. 28), and the statement concerning Christ, " In Him all things consist (or, hold together) " (Col. i. 17). There is also a striking saying, not recorded in our Gospels, but early attributed to Jesus: " Raise the stone, and there thou shalt find Me ; cleave the wood, and there am I."

This idea of God's Indwelling is most fully expressed in Wordsworth's well-known lines:

> And I have felt
> A presence that disturbs me with the joy
> Of elevated thoughts ; a sense sublime
> Of something far more deeply interfused,
> Whose dwelling is the light of setting suns,
> And the round ocean, and the living air,
> And the blue sky, and in the mind of man ;
> A motion and a spirit, that impels
> All thinking things, all objects of all thought,
> And rolls through all things.

But Christianity differs from Pantheism in combining with this doctrine of the Immanence, or Indwelling, of God the doctrine of His *Transcendence.* By this we mean that God not only dwells in the world, but exists apart from the Universe as Lord and Ruler over all things. The God of the Bible is " the high and lofty One, that inhabiteth eternity " (Isa. lvii. 15) ; and " His kingdom ruleth over all " (Ps. ciii. 19).

4. *God is Eternal.* It goes without saying that, if there is a God, He must be eternal: He can have had no beginning. For otherwise we should have to assume the existence of some other Being, prior to Him, to account for His beginning. Not much is gained by attempting to picture to our minds what is meant by the statement, " From everlasting to everlasting, Thou art God " (Ps. xc. 2). All that we can say is, that God *always* was, and *always* will be. However far back we may travel in thought, God existed then ; and, however far forward we may travel in thought, God will still exist then.

5. *God is Unchangeable.* If God is eternal, the lapse of time can produce no change in Him. His existence cannot be measured in time: for Him a thousand years are as one day (see Ps. xc. 4), in the sense that both the thousand years and the one day are insignificantly small when compared with eternity. Perhaps the best way of stating the unchangeableness of God is to say that an eternal Being can never grow older: after millions of years of existence He is no nearer the end of His Being. All else changes and decays, but God abides: cf. " I the Lord change not " (Mal. iii. 6), and " I am the Alpha and the Omega, the beginning and the end " (Rev. xxi. 6). God never changes in His might and never wearies in His purposes.

> O mighty God, Thy matchless power
> Is ever *new* and ever *young*,
> And firm endures, while endless years
> Their everlasting circles run.

6. *God is Almighty or Omnipotent.* It is almost impossible to think of God as the God of the Universe without ascribing to Him almighty power: power less than almighty would not be adequate for the creation and maintenance of such a Universe. It is not of much use to try to picture to ourselves His might ; it is sufficient to say He has all the power requisite for the needs of the Universe, or of any Universe that He may choose to make. The fact that He has made and does sustain the present Universe is all the proof that is needed. Hence we may say that God can do whatever He will, or that " with God all things are possible " (Matt. xix. 26).

This does not mean, however, that we cannot conceive things which God cannot do. He cannot do the self-contradictory or absurd. For instance, He cannot make a square circle or an aged infant. Similarly, there are some things which are morally impossible: God cannot make wrong right, or right wrong ; in other words, " He cannot deny Himself " (2 Tim. ii. 13).

7. *God is everywhere or Omnipresent.* The God of the

Universe must necessarily be equally present in all parts of the Universe. If Creation depends on Him entirely, as it does, there is no part of the Universe that does not need His incessant activity and care. Not that we are to picture to ourselves God diffused over all space like an atmosphere. The truth is rather that, for pure, unfettered Spirit, space can have no meaning: all places are equally near and equally far off, and God can *act* equally readily everywhere. Even in our own experience, space can be to some extent annihilated: our thought and affection may be on the far side of the globe while our bodies are here ; and there seems to be some evidence that, even in the case of human beings, influence can be exerted at a distance by transference of thought.

8. *God knows all things, or is Omniscient.* It is clear that a spiritual God, who has made all things and is present everywhere, must know all things, that is, everything that there is to be known. We may consider God's knowledge under three headings.

(*a*) In relation to *Creation* God's knowledge is called *Wisdom*. As Ruler of the Universe, seeing all things in their completeness, His plans and purposes must be perfectly clear to Him even when they seem least intelligible to us. We are, therefore, bound to believe that whatever He wills is best. We ourselves are but little creatures, hardly more capable of grasping the great purposes of God than the fly which flits from point to point in a vast cathedral is capable of comprehending the complete design of the architect. It is not surprising that God's thoughts are not our thoughts (see Isa. lv. 8, 9) ; and we can only say of His works, " In wisdom hast Thou made them all " (Ps. civ. 24).

(*b*) In relation to the *individual man* God's knowledge is *knowledge of the heart*. If He is an Infinite Spirit, present everywhere, no secret recess of our hearts can be hidden from His sight. To use the old words of the Catechism, " God knows all things ; every thought in man's heart, every word, and every action " (see Ps.

cxxxix. 2 - 4).   As will be seen later, this truth has important consequences:

(i) To satisfy such a God, there must be inward as well as outward purity.

(ii) The God who knows us altogether, and He alone, will be able to judge us with perfect justice.

(c) In relation to the *future* God's knowledge is *foreknowledge*. It is clear that God, being what He is, must know all things beforehand (see Isa. xlvi. 10). This raises the old difficulty that, if God knows what we shall do or become, our actions and destiny must be determined in advance, and we cannot really be free.   The subject of Man's Free Will is treated more fully later, but here we may point out that what God foreknows is what men will do, *acting of their own free will*.   Foreknowledge does not determine action: we ourselves know beforehand that the sun will rise at a particular time on a given day, but our foreknowledge does not cause it to do so.

B.—ATTRIBUTES OF GOD REVEALED IN THE BIBLE ONLY.

We come now to consider further attributes of God that would not be known to us apart from the Bible.

1. *God is Holy*.   For us the idea of Holiness is now so bound up with the name of God, that we find it difficult to imagine that He could ever have been conceived of in any other way.   But the heathen neighbours of Israel, like the heathen nations of to-day, believed not only in gods many, but in gods wicked and immoral.   Of all those mentioned in Scripture, not one was a god of character : they were monsters of lust, cruelty and spite.   Children were burnt in sacrifice to Moloch, and impurity actually formed part of the worship of Astarte and some others.

Next to the stress laid on God's Unity, much the most important item in the O.T. teaching about God is His Holiness.   " Be ye *holy,* for I am *holy* " (Lev. xi. 44), was a new way of thinking of both God and His service.

In other religions the gods were served partly by sacrifices and partly by abominable rites, but there was no sort of connexion between religion and moral conduct. The Ten Commandments, which set forth the service of God in a series of *moral* precepts, though they seem to us so obvious, must have come as a startlingly novel revelation. It was the vision of God's Holiness that made Isaiah a prophet (Isa. vi. 3), and that Holiness formed the burden of his message.

Outside the Bible we find our belief in God's Holiness confirmed:

(1) By the beauty and perfection of His works (see pp. 12, 13),

(2) By His influence in History, as making for righteousness (see p. 14).

For us the significance of God's Holiness is two-fold:

(1) It makes holiness a part of any religion by which we are to please God. Henceforth piety and morality are wedded together.

(2) It encourages all who are working to promote righteousness in the community: the God of the Universe is on their side. It might conceivably have been otherwise: God might have been an evil God, and in struggling for righteousness we might have had to contend against Him and against the whole trend of His Universe. As it is, there is the " Power not ourselves that makes for righteousness," and we can sing:

> For right is right, since God is God,
>   And right the day must win ;
> To doubt would be disloyalty,
>   To falter would be sin.

2. *God is merciful and gracious.* (*a*) *Mercy*. The Old Testament continually represents God as being *merciful* in His Sovereignty over men. More particularly it speaks of Him as considerate and forbearing towards their sins and short-comings, a God of long-suffering and forgiveness (see Ex. xx. 6 ; Ps. ciii. 17).

(*b*) *Grace*. The Old Testament also describes God as *gracious* (see Neh. ix. 17 ; Ps. cxi. 4) ; but the beautiful word *grace* is more distinctive of the New Testament. It was used in Classical Greek for gracefulness of person or of movement, and for the graciousness of a superior towards his inferiors ; but in the New Testament it is consecrated to higher uses, and is reserved exclusively for the free and undeserved mercy of *God*. God's whole attitude towards sinful men is one of grace ; but the supreme instance of His grace is found in " His unspeakable gift " of His Son, and the free and unreserved forgiveness of sin as the result of the Atonement (see Rom. v. 15 ; Eph. ii. 7 ; 1 Pet. v. 10).

3. *God is love*. No statement concerning God could possibly be simpler or more attractive than that " God is love " (1 John iv. 8) ; yet none seems, at times, more difficult to believe. To judge from human love, the Love of God must mean that God is eager to make men truly happy ; and that He is eager to possess them for His own.

(1) *God's Love as Concern for Men's Welfare*

The Bible teaches that *God cares for the happiness of men* individually (Matt. vi. 30 - 33), even when they are ungrateful and unworthy (Matt. v. 45). This is the doctrine that makes Christianity the most comforting of all religions. Outside the Bible this belief finds support in:

- (*a*) The numberless joys that come to men unsought and undeserved ;
- (*b*) The many kinds of pleasure that human nature is fitted to enjoy and our world is able to provide ;
- (*c*) The beauty of the earth, sea and sky.

Objection : Suffering and Sorrow. The difficulty presented by the *Problem of Suffering and Sorrow* is a very serious one. Nature often seems cruel: diseases like cancer, disasters such as earthquakes and hurricanes, and the ruthless preying of the strong upon the weak among the animals, make it very difficult to believe in the goodness of God.

To deal first with *the suffering of the animal world*, it is only fair to say that it is often exaggerated. Sooner or later all animals must die, and to fall a prey to others generally results in a swift and comparatively painless death. It is very doubtful whether pain is as intense for animals as for human beings, and in their case it is not prolonged by anticipation in imagination. Again, the preying of species upon species makes it possible for the world to sustain a vastly larger number of living creatures, and a vastly greater variety of life, than would otherwise be possible ; and, on the whole, life is pleasant, as is seen in. the case of the lambs and the birds. Further, Nature provides by this very means what we may call an automatic system of sanitation, so that the air is not polluted by the products of animal decay.

But the most important consideration is that the Bible maintains that *sin has blighted the world,* and brought in its train suffering for animals as well as for men (see Rom. viii. 19-22).

Turning now to consider *suffering and sorrow as they are found amongst men,* it is well to remember that the Bible nowhere represents God as amiably and weakly indulgent. His Love is a *moral* love, that cannot ignore sin, and that cherishes high and lofty purposes for men : to be a loving God He need not resemble a fond and foolish mother.

There are two main considerations that will help us:

(*a*) *Pain is often a safe-guard to life and health.* The pain of burning is meant as a warning ; for, if it caused no pain, our flesh might be burnt through to the bone before we were aware of danger. The pain of inflammation and fever is the result of Nature's effort to throw off disease and save our lives.

(*b*) *Suffering and sorrow are two of the greatest moral influences in life.*

(i) Pain, disease and misery are often the punishment of the sufferer's own sin and folly, and so serve as a corrective and a warning against sin.

(ii) Want, hardship, and sorrow are often the consequence of the sin or injustice of others, and are not the direct will of God. If it be said that a good God could not allow the innocent to suffer through the fault of the guilty, it may be replied that, if undeserved suffering comes to men through others, undeserved happiness also comes to them through others. Further, the fact that we are linked together, so that a mother can suffer through the sin of her son, or a child through the sin of his father, gives men a solemn sense of responsibility for their actions, and often serves to hold them back from sins which they would otherwise commit.

(iii) Suffering and sorrow may be " purging fires " to purify and refine the character of the sufferer. The purest and sweetest characters are produced by suffering apparently undeserved, and true humility and spirituality are often the outcome of great loss, disappointment, or sorrow.

(iv) Suffering and sorrow call forth tenderness and sympathy in others. An invalid wife or a cripple child may be " a minister of God for good " to a hard and selfish man by continually appealing to his sympathy and consideration. But for the presence of want and sorrow the world would be far harder and more selfish than it is. It is suffering that has developed all the charities and philanthropies. And, if the lot of such innocent sufferers seems hard, they have the consolation of knowing that they exercise a very gracious influence—they suffer that others may be made kind and tender ; and even the agony of cancer may not be too much to endure for such an end as that.

(v) It is also hinted in Scripture that the angels are spectators of the drama of human life: cf. the opening chapter of the Book of Job, and such sayings as, " Which things angels desire to look into " (1 Peter i. 12). If this be so, human endurance may even have its lessons for these unseen spectators.

There is little suffering that cannot be accounted for in one or other of these ways. For the rest, we must remember that, according to the Bible, we do not see the world as God meant it to be in His original purpose of love, but as *cursed by sin* (see Gen. iii. 16 - 19) ; and also that we are such little creatures that God's purpose may be right and loving, even when it seems cruel to us. In the religious life we have to walk by *faith*, not by sight ; and it is in such matters as these that we have to show the reality of our faith. To abandon belief in a good God only leaves the mystery greater than before, and deprives us of the one hope that gives consolation to the sufferer. What we know and understand of God shows Him to be so far good that it is only just to Him to believe that He is always " too wise to err, too good to be unkind."

> Thy judgments are a mighty deep
> Beyond all fathom-line ;
> Our wisdom is the childlike heart,
> Our strength to trust in Thine.

(2) *God's Love as Desire for the Love of Men*

The second aspect of the Love of God mentioned on p. 34 was that *God seeks to possess men for His own* in loving communion. This is the doctrine that makes Christianity the most inspiring and ennobling of religions, for it shows to the vilest and most degraded the hope of better possibilities, and gives to them a sense of worth and dignity, since they are precious in God's sight.

It is found in the Old Testament, especially in some of the pathetic pleadings of the prophets, such as Hos. xi. 1-4 and 8. But it runs through and through the New Testament, and is, indeed the " good news " of the Gospel.

(*a*) It is supremely manifested in Jesus Christ, God's " unspeakable gift."

(*b*) The purpose for which Christ came was to seek the lost and reconcile them to God (see Luke xix. 10 and 2 Cor. v. 19.).

(*c*) Christ's whole attitude towards the sinful and the outcast was meant to teach God's loving purpose.

(*d*) Many of His most striking parables have this for their theme, especially the great trio in Luke xv.

(*e*) This love of God was the origin of Christ's redeeming work (see John iii. 16 and Rom. v. 8).

(*f*) It is the explanation of all Christian character (see Gal. ii. 20), and of the Christian's love for God (see 1 John iv. 19).

4. *God is our Father.* Fatherhood is hardly a separate attribute of God, but it is an important part of the New Testament revelation of Him, and it is convenient to treat the subject in close connexion with His Love.

In the doctrine of God's Fatherhood we add to His Love the thought that He loves us because we are *related to Him as His children.* There are many kinds of love besides that of a father for his child. Here the Love of God is based on the fact we derive our life from Him (Acts xvii. 28). It is in keeping with this that we are told in Gen. i. 27 that Man was made in the image of God.

The word " Father " is used of God in several senses:

(*a*) In the Old Testament He is the Father of the nation of Israel (see Isa. lxiii. 16).

(*b*) In such passages as John xiv. 10, 11, and throughout John xvii., He is the Father of Jesus in a sense in which He is not the Father of men. So, too, in the phrase " the God and Father of our Lord Jesus Christ," which occurs frequently in the Epistles.

(*c*) In the Sermon on the Mount (e.g., Matt. vi. 4, 14, 15, 32, etc.) He is the Father of all men.

(*d*) In a higher sense He is the Father of believers. By faith in Christ we become sons of God in a special sense (John i. 12), and this sonship gives us the right to use the name Father with special freedom (see Rom. viii. 15).

The difference between (*c*) and (*d*) may be compared to the difference between the nominal sonship of one who has abandoned his home and is utterly out of sympathy with his father, and the real sonship of one who prizes the relationship and is living in glad enjoyment of his father's affection.

Two very important consequences follow from belief in the Fatherhood of God:

(1) Belief in God's Providence ; (2) Belief in Prayer.

(1) *Providence*

If God is our Father, it is natural to believe that *He feels an interest in our individual welfare and provides for our wants*. Some recognize a General Providence, which cares for the Race or the Church, but do not admit a Personal Providence, which cares for individuals.

The doctrine is found in Old Testament (see 2 Chron. xvi. 9 ; Ps. xxvii. 10, ciii. 13). In the teaching of Jesus the care of God is represented as extending to the minutest details of our life (Matt. x. 30), and throughout the Sermon on the Mount it is described as the outcome of His Fatherly love.

The objections urged against this belief are:

(*a*) The presence of *sorrow and suffering* in the world, especially the suffering of the innocent. This difficulty has been dealt with on pp. 34—37.

(*b*) The *insignificance of man,* which, it is said, makes it inconceivable that God can care for him individually.

Sometimes it is urged that Man at best is a little creature, *beneath God's consideration*. Yet the microscope reveals infinite care, skill and perfection of finish in the structure of creatures immeasurably smaller than Man. And if we bear in mind Man's moral and spiritual nature, he cannot be measured simply in feet or pounds. Love knows nothing of size: a baby is more lovable than a mountain.

Or, again, it may be urged that the individual man is only one out of hundreds of millions, and that, whilst God may care for the Race, He cannot distinguish the needs of *individuals*. It is probably true that where the interests of the individual clash with those of the Race, the larger interests must come first. A father puts the general welfare of the family above that of the individual child, and we have no reason to suppose that the World is ordered primarily for the happiness of any individual.

Indeed, many individuals perish in the progress of the Race, e.g., in scientific experiments, exploration, or the introduction of new arts, such as aviation. Yet an earthly father also knows his children individually and cares for them separately, not merely as a family. And if we think of the hundreds of men whom any one of us knows, and in whom we feel a measure of personal interest, why should it be a thing inconceivable that the Infinite God should know and care for the millions of mankind?

(2) *Prayer*

The second natural consequence of belief in the Fatherhood of God is belief in *Prayer*. Under this we include *Communion with God,* which must obviously be possible if God desires to possess us for His own in loving fellowship, as stated on p. 34 ; and *Petition,* or the asking for gifts.

Is this latter kind of prayer possible? Is it true that if we ask we shall receive? If God is really our Father, such petitions seem natural, and the teaching of the Bible is unquestionably that such prayer avails (see Matt. vii. 7 ; John xvi. 23 ; Phil. iv. 6, 7 ; James v. 16). There are countless instances in which it is affirmed that such prayers, even prayers for material things, have been answered, as in the case of Müller's Orphanage, of which it is said that from its foundation all its funds have come in answer to prayer.

The first objection often urged is that *the Universe is one of law and order,* and that we cannot suppose that God will intervene to alter the natural succession of events. To suggest that God *cannot* intervene is to reduce Him to a weakness greater than our own, for we can and do modify the order of many events by the action of our own wills. Very often this objection is based on the supposition that God can only intervene by *violating* the existing laws of Nature. The Christian reply is that we ourselves change the course of things by *using* the laws and the powers of Nature, not by violating them. The doctor performs his cures by using drugs according to the laws of Nature ; and the engineer executes his wonders by using natural forces, such as steam and electricity, according to the laws of Nature. And the more we know of Nature, the greater becomes our power to use its forces for our own ends. But if we, with our limited knowledge, can do this, the God who knows the Universe perfectly must be able to intervene and modify the course of events continually without violating any law of Nature.

A second and more weighty objection to belief in Prayer is that *God, in His love and wisdom, must necessarily will what is best for us,* and is not to be turned from His purpose by our pleading. But Christianity does not teach that Prayer alters the will of God—a fundamental condition of all successful prayer is that it should be "according to the will of God." The uses we claim for Prayer are these:

(i) There is relief in the very process of making known our needs and our difficulties to a sympathizing Friend.

(ii) It is a fitting and seemly thing that a child should acknowledge his dependence on the bounty of his father by asking. There are blessings which God's love prompts Him to bestow, but which He cannot rightly give to us so long as our hearts are proud and independent. The spirit of humble petition makes it possible for Him to give them.

(iii) Many of the best things of life, such as knowledge, can only be imparted to those who are eager to receive and willing to do their part in the work of receiving. This is specially true of the spiritual gifts, and in prayer for these we are taking in what God cannot give without our co-operation.

(iv) There are indications that Thought and Will are positive *forces*. Now all the minds of the Universe meet in God, just as all the telephone wires of a great city meet at the Central Exchange. May we not suppose that the expression of earnest need, going out from the heart of some poverty-stricken woman, *passes through God* to reach the heart of some one able to help, and creates in him the impulse to help her? In the same way the love

of a mother for her son and her earnest desire for his good
may reach him through God in the form of blessing.

Prayer is nowhere represented as a miraculous charm,
or a substitute for work that we can do ourselves: it is
rather a linking ourselves up with God, and so making
use of the vast unseen forces of His Universe. Hence the
conditions of prayer are earnestness, faith, obedience to
God, and submission to His will ; for it is only by these
means that we can link ourselves to God.

5. *God is a Trinity in Unity*. This topic is often
treated after the subjects of Jesus Christ and the Holy
Spirit. But it is such a unique feature in the Bible teaching about God that it is introduced here for the sake of
completeness.

Nature and the Bible agree in teaching that God is One.
Christianity further teaches that in that Unity there are
Three " Persons," Father, Son, and Holy Spirit. This
is a doctrine that is taught only by Christianity. Even in
the Bible it is not so much stated in explicit terms as
implied. It should be noted, however, that it is not the
outcome of mere speculation, but is based on the three
different ways in which God has manifested Himself in
man's experience.

The reasons for framing such a doctrine were that:

(1) In the New Testament the Father, the Son, and the
Holy Spirit are repeatedly spoken of as separate
" Persons," each of them divine. We have, therefore, to
believe either in the Trinity or in Three Gods.

(2) In the formula of Baptism (Matt. xxviii. 19) " the
Name of the Father and of the Son and of the Holy Ghost "
is *one* Name. The Three " Persons " are also associated
together in *one* blessing in the Benediction (2 Cor. xiii. 14).

We are, therefore, shut up to the doctrine of the Trinity.
Those who deny it can only do so by denying the Divinity
of Christ, and are called *Unitarians*. The reply to their
case is the argument for the Divinity of Christ, which is
dealt with on pp. 55—65.

The inner meaning of the doctrine is difficult to state, and no figure used to illustrate it is altogether satisfactory. A comparison is sometimes made, for instance, with the three elements that make up man's inner life: feeling, thinking, and willing. But, though these three make one mind, they are not always in harmony.

The doctrine is that while God is One, there are in Him three distinguishable centres of Love, Thought and Will, that is, Three "Persons," exercising different functions but always acting in perfect harmony. The difficulty arises mainly from the fact that our English word "person" does not represent what the first Christian thinkers meant when they chose the Latin word *persona*. That was used, for instance, for a "character" on the stage, and it was not uncommon for one player to represent three different characters. Probably we can safely go no further than Dr. Newton Clarke's expression of the doctrine, "God is a Person, in whose nature there is a threeness that has been expressed in His three-fold self-manifestation."

The doctrine of the Trinity, however, throws light on two important facts:

(1) It explains how in the history and redemption of Mankind God has manifested Himself in Three Persons, each of them divine: the Father as Sovereign, the Son as Saviour, the Spirit as Sanctifier.

(2) It explains how God might exist in bliss before there was any Universe upon which to spend His love. A heart with absolutely nothing to love, and a mind with absolutely nothing outside itself to exercise itself upon, could hardly be said to live. Yet, if God is not a bare, cold Unity, but a Trinity, we can conceive how each of the Three Persons might find a full and perfect life in the love of the others and in communion with them, before the world began. There is a parallel to this in the fact that Man can hold communion with himself. And the perfecting of the love of husband and wife by their common love for their

child suggests that the love of Two Persons in the Trinity for each other might be made complete in their common love for the Third.

CHAPTER IV

THE CHRISTIAN BELIEF CONCERNING JESUS AND ITS JUSTIFICATION

THE very foundation of the Christian Religion is its belief concerning Jesus. This may be stated in the familiar words of the Apostles' Creed:

Jesus Christ His only Son our Lord, Who was conceived by the Holy Ghost, Born of the Virgin Mary, suffered under Pontius Pilate, Was crucified, dead, and buried, He descended into hell; The third day He rose again from the dead, He ascended into heaven, And sitteth on the right hand of God the Father Almighty; From thence He shall come to judge the quick and the dead.

It is impossible to imagine any greater claim than is implied in these words, every one of which is important.

It should be noted that the claim for Jesus is stated in a series of *facts,* for Christianity is a *historic* religion, i.e., it is not the outcome of speculation, but is bound up with the Person of Christ and the facts of His life and work. It would make little or no difference to the truth or falsity of Buddhism or Confucianism if the current beliefs concerning their founders were disproved. But, if the main facts of the story of Jesus can be disproved, the Christian system collapses; for the faith of a Christian is not merely belief in Christ's teaching, but trust in Christ Himself, His merits and Death. It is, therefore, of the utmost importance to feel sure that we have the right to believe in the principal facts recorded concerning Him.

A.—ARE OUR RECORDS TRUSTWORTHY?

The story of the life of Christ has come down to us in four short memoirs, the *Gospels*. For our present purpose there is no need to claim for them absolute harmony or infallible accuracy ; it is enough to show that their general story of the life of Jesus can be trusted.

The Fourth Gospel has been more disputed than the other three, though modern opinion is much more favourable to it than the critics were forty to fifty years ago. Moreover, it was written with a theological purpose (see John xx. 31), and not as a simple narrative. We shall do best, therefore, to consider only the three " Synoptics," Matthew, Mark and Luke.

When we compare these together, we are struck with the fact that very nearly the whole of Mark is substantially reproduced in Matthew and Luke ; and that in these portions the three agree in the selection of facts, in their general order, and often even in language. There are, however, points of difference that rule out most of the simpler theories of the relation of the three. But it seems certain that Mark was written first, and highly probable that he was used by both " Matthew " and Luke, who also had further sources of information. But, before any Gospel was written, the story of Jesus was known among Christian disciples in the form of the *Oral Tradition*, which was taught from memory.

It seems that in *Mark* we have this Oral Tradition committed to writing. But there is evidence that St. Mark wrote under the direction of St. Peter, so that in this Gospel we have the story of Jesus as it was commonly accepted within about thirty-five years of the Death of Christ, revised according to the personal reminiscences of one of the most intimate of the disciples.

Matthew gives us no clue to its authorship, and the tradition which ascribes it to St. Matthew is only poorly supported. There is, however, good evidence that the Apostle made a collection of *Logia*, or Sayings of Jesus, and it is almost certain that these are included in this Gospel ; so that the name of St. Matthew may have been attached to it on that account. Such collections of sayings are found in the Sermon on the Mount, chapters v-vii, and in the parables of chapter xiii. In this Gospel we have, therefore, the same general narrative as in Mark, with the addition of the story of the Birth of Jesus and much teaching of Jesus not recorded there; and in all probability the teaching, at least, is supported by the special authority of St. Matthew, one of the Twelve.

St. Luke is a witness of special interest and value. (1) He was the intimate friend of St. Paul, so that his testimony carries with it that of St. Paul and of the many early witnesses with whom he would come into contact through St. Paul. (2) He was a physician, a man of education, and therefore not likely to accept any statement without good evidence. (3) In the Acts he shows himself to be an exceedingly careful and accurate historian. Sir William Ramsay devoted his life to the study of the history of Asia Minor during the first century. He started on his first tour of exploration, as a young man, with the belief that St. Luke was quite untrustworthy. He found, however, such remarkable evidence of minute accuracy in his references to the regions traversed by St. Paul, that he ended by declaring that he was a historian of the very first rank. (4) St. Luke solemnly declares in the preface to his Gospel (i. 1 - 4) that he had been at special pains to ensure the strict accuracy of his narrative.

The case may, therefore, be summed up thus:

(*a*) The story of the Ministry, Death and Resurrection of Jesus comes to us in substantially the same form from *three* writers, who yet show considerable independence.

(*b*) It has also the sanction of St. Peter and St. Paul, and their circles of acquaintances.

(*c*) It represents an Oral Tradition, current before any Gospel was written. Further, this had assumed an almost stereotyped form by the time St. Mark wrote, about A.D. 66, i.e., within less than forty years of the Crucifixion. At this date there must have been many eye-witnesses still living, and there had not been time for legend to grow up.

Even earlier than the written Gospels are some of the *Epistles*. The genuineness of the greatest of these, namely, Romans, 1 and 2 Corinthians, and Galatians, is admitted almost without dispute ; and they not only refer to the Ministry, Death and Resurrection of Jesus, but treat them as facts already perfectly familiar to Gentile Christians far from Palestine.

The evidence for the general narrative is, in short, so strong that, if it is not reliable, there is no fact of history on which we can rely.

B.—SOME SPECIAL DIFFICULTIES IN THE NARRATIVE

There are three facts in the Gospel story which are so beset with difficulty as to require separate treatment.

1. *The Virgin Birth*. This is not one of the essential doctrines of Christianity: men may, and in fact some do, believe in the Incarnation, whilst rejecting this mystery.

Apart from its miraculous character, the only arguments urged against it are that there is no reference to it in either Mark or John ; and that it is not mentioned either in the Epistles or in the sermons recorded in Acts.

To this we may reply that:

(1) St. Mark begins his Gospel with the Ministry of Jesus, not with His Birth ; and St. John wrote his to supplement, not to repeat, what was already known.

(2) The subject was necessarily a delicate one ; and, so long as Mary lived, it would be difficult to refer to it.

(3) The Evangelists never speak of Joseph as the father of Jesus, though His neighbours and opponents sometimes did so.

(4) The peculiar phrase, " *made* of a woman " (Gal. iv. 4), seems to imply that St. Paul was acquainted with the mystery. This is not admitted by all, and the R.V. translates the phrase " *born* of a woman." But the word for " born " is unusual in that sense.

(5) It is difficult to account for the rise of the story if it was not true.

(6) It harmonizes well with the mystery of the Incarnation that the Son of God should be born in a way other than the ordinary.

On the whole, it is easier to accept the doctrine than to reject it. To reject it does not lessen the difficulty of believing in the Incarnation, and seriously discredits two of our Gospels without any corresponding gain.

2. *The Miracles of Jesus.* There are some who find an obstacle to faith in the miraculous element in the Gospels.

(*a*) For those who believe in God miracles are *not* to be ruled out as *impossible*. As shown on p. 40, a miracle does not imply a *violation* of the laws of Nature ; it may be merely God's way of *using* the laws and forces of Nature. In many of His works of healing, our Lord seems to do swiftly and easily what our doctors do painfully and slowly. It is possible that, if they knew as much of the secrets of Nature as He did, their cures might be as swift and easy as His.

(*b*) If miracles are possible, they would be *most appropriate in a new revelation* of God, and there could be no more fitting occasion for them than in the Ministry of the Son of God. If Jesus was the Son of God, it would have been strange if He had not worked miracles.

(*c*) The miracles of Jesus always appear to be *simple* and *dignified* in character. The grotesque stories of vulgar wonder-working which occur in the Apocryphal Gospels, such as giving life to clay birds, are not found in our Gospels.

(*d*) With the exception of the matter of the Gadarene Swine and the Withering of the Fig tree, on which commentaries should be consulted, our Lord's miracles were *works of mercy*. He appears never to have used His powers to secure His own comfort or safety, but used them freely to relieve others. It is difficult to see how He could have made a complete revelation of love without doing so.

(*e*) The New Testament narratives *could not be myths,* for the interval between the death of Jesus and the first written references to His miracles was not sufficient to allow of the growth of myths. And the fantastic apocryphal stories which grew up later show us the type of miracle that we should have had if our Gospels were myths.

3. *The Resurrection.* The consequences of the Resurrection of Jesus in Christian Doctrine will be considered in the next chapter. Here we shall deal only with question of fact, *Did Jesus rise from the dead?* This question is of absolutely vital importance to Christianity.

(1) *The Positive Testimony*

Let us consider first the positive testimony.

(*a*) The story is recorded with considerable detail in all four Gospels ; and St. Paul names in 1 Cor. xv. 5 - 8 a list of witnesses, many of whom were still living at the time he wrote. If there are small discrepancies in the Gospel accounts, they do not weaken the force of their testimony to the fact itself, any more than minor variations in the newspaper descriptions of a great public event cause us to question its reality.

(*b*) The very existence of the Christian Church at all is a proof that the Resurrection actually took place. The disciples were reduced by the Crucifixion to absolute despair. But something happened that transformed them, and created in their hearts an unalterable conviction that Jesus had returned from tne grave. If He had not risen, the Church would have been buried with Him.

(*c*) The belief became so central with the early Church, that the first day of the week was to them henceforth " the Lord's Day," i.e., the day of Jesus, the risen Lord ; and eventually took the place of the Sabbath as their day of rest and worship. Every returning Sunday is evidence of the reality of the Resurrection.

(*d*) The Resurrection, even more than the Atonement, was the great theme of Apostolic preaching, as is seen in the sermons of St. Peter and St. Paul recorded in the Acts. The Apostles gloried in the fact that they were "witnesses." And this preaching began, not after the lapse of many years, when a myth might have had time to grow up, or in distant lands, where it could not be contradicted, but immediately and in Jerusalem itself. It would instantly have been disproved, if the Body could have been shown in the tomb. But there appears to have been no serious attempt either to deny that the grave was empty, or to account for the fact that it was so.

(2) *Alternative Theories*

We may now consider the theories that have been advanced from time to time to explain away the fact of the Resurrection, and to account for the evident conviction of the disciples. They are almost pathetic in their failure.

(*a*) A favourite theory from early times onwards has been that Jesus did not really die upon the Cross, but *swooned* and was taken down for dead ; that in the coolness of the tomb He revived, and so made His way out, and appeared to His disciples. It was to guard against this theory that the apparently superfluous word "dead" was inserted in the Apostles' Creed, "crucified, *dead,* and buried." The objections are obvious:

(i) It is expressly mentioned that Pilate provided against this contingency by his order that the side of Jesus should be pierced.

(ii) If the theory were true, how could Jesus, recovering from his swoon, roll away the great stone and escape the Roman guards? Or, if He escaped, weak and wounded as He would be, how could He impress His disciples as having triumphed over death, and kindle their enthusiasm? He would be an invalid, needing weeks of rest and nursing.

(iii) If Jesus did not die on Calvary, when and where did He die?

(*b*) Some have maintained that the disciples' belief arose from an *hallucination :* that Mary, nervous and overwrought, imagined that she saw Jesus near the tomb, and declared to the rest that He was risen. But this theory is quite as unsatisfactory as the last, for:

(i) Hallucinations are likely to occur only when an event is eagerly longed for and expected. But the disciples were altogether unprepared for the Resurrection. For the most part they were prosaic, healthy-minded men, and nothing was further from their thoughts than that Jesus could rise again. Indeed, Thomas stoutly refused to believe, even on the testimony of many witnesses.

(ii) The theory assumes that the hallucinations somehow became contagious, and lasted for several weeks, affecting hundreds of persons.

(iii) It does not explain how or why these hallucinations ever ceased.

(iv) It does not explain how the grave came to be empty.

(c) A rather ingenious theory is that what the disciples saw was *a vision of Christ in Heaven,* and that they received from Him a message that it was well with Him. This might, perhaps, explain the revival of their faith and enthusiasm, but:

(i) It does not account for the empty grave.

(ii) It admits the reality of the spiritual and the supernatural, and so might equally well admit the miracle of the Resurrection.

(iii) It discredits the Gospel narrative without any corresponding gain.

We are shut up to accepting the Resurrection as an actual fact:

(i) Because nothing less can explain the change in the disciples.

(ii) Because it does not seem to have been seriously denied at the time.

(iii) Because no other theory accounts for the rise of the Gospel story. In short, it is more difficult to reject the miracle than to accept it.

C.—THE GOSPEL PORTRAIT OF JESUS

The character of Jesus as sketched in the Gospels is so unique that many consider it quite as miraculous as any of the works associated with His name. If Jesus is not a miracle of fact, the Gospel story is a miracle of imagination.

The life and character of Jesus become the more impressive when we consider His *surroundings* and the *times* in which He lived.

He was brought up in a humble artisan home. He can have had little education ; and there is nothing in what we read of Mary, Joseph, and the rest of that family circle, to account for such a religious genius.

Nazareth was an obscure and commonplace village, with a mongrel population and, perhaps, an evil reputation.

The Jewish nation was decaying: its liberty was gone, the heroic days lay in the distant past, and the life of the country had become stagnant. Even religion had lost its freshness and vitality, and was represented chiefly by formal Pharisees and sceptical and worldly Sadducees. There was, indeed, John the Baptist as a prophet ; but he does not explain the life and ministry of Jesus, he only announced its beginning.

We have thus the extraordinary fact that the most beautiful and complete character the world has ever known, the one which sums up in itself all the highest we can conceive of human life, appeared suddenly amongst surroundings that were in almost every way unfavourable.

Many different elements enter into the *character* of Jesus. We shall try to distinguish them, but the whole is more beautiful than any of its parts. Many noble men and women have possessed a few graces of character in a high degree, but Jesus possessed them *all* in the *highest* degree.

1. *Sinlessness.* Of Jesus, and of Him alone, has it ever been said that "He did no sin, neither was guile found in His mouth" (1 Peter ii. 22) ; and that "He hath been in all points tempted like as we are yet without

sin " (Heb. iv. 15). No other saint has ever lived who was not conscious of guilt, and who had not to pray for forgiveness. That the life of Jesus, as sketched in the Gospels, was really free from sin, is shown by the fact that few have ever attempted to criticize it, and none has succeeded in pointing out any real flaw.

2. The character of Jesus was more than innocent, it was *actively and bravely good*. His virtues were not those of the monk or the hermit: He lived a strenuous life, in close touch with men, facing many hardships and temptations. He " went about doing good " (Acts x. 38), and His virtue was of the practical kind that commends itself to the man of the world: He lived a busy life, crowded with travelling, teaching, and works of mercy ; and He did this at great cost to Himself. He was poor and homeless, but there is no trace of any desire for self-aggrandizement or even self-protection. The powers He used for the benefit of others He refused to use for Himself. His life was one of continual self-sacrifice.

3. Jesus is the supreme example of *pity* for men in their needs and sorrows, and of, what is rarer than pity, actual *love* of men for their own sakes. He saw something precious and lovable in the vilest, and—painful as the association must sometimes have been—became the Friend of the sinful and the despised. He possessed the love which " hopeth all things," and consistently believed in the better possibilities latent in the most degraded of men and women. The Persian legend, which describes Him as finding beauty in the white teeth of a foul dead dog, indicates how this trait in His character has impressed men.

4. The character of Jesus, however, was not lacking in sterner and robuster qualities. His tenderness was not incompatible with an intense *hatred of sin,* and He was capable of a noble indignation against hypocrisy, meanness, and injustice.

5. He made many foes and His life was frequently in danger. It must have required no small *courage* to continue a work that often appeared hopeless ; and we are

told that " He steadfastly set His face to go to Jerusalem,'' where He knew that death awaited Him.

6. Human life cannot reach its highest without some *purpose* or *ambition*. Jesus seems to have been conscious of a great mission, and to this He gave Himself absolutely. His aim was one of perfect obedience to the will of the Father, whatever the cost might be.

7. No life can be conceived more deeply *spiritual* than that of Jesus. He was always conscious of dependence upon God, and lived in closest fellowship with Heaven. Prayer was unspeakably precious to Him, and, on occasion, " He continued all night in prayer " (Luke vi. 12).

8. On any view of His Nature, Jesus shows a *spiritual insight* that is quite unique. (1) This is seen in His teaching about God and the unseen world. Whether men accept this or not, they cannot deny that it is always consistent and worthy of a great God ; a teaching that they wish could be true, even while they reject it. (2) It is seen in His knowledge of the hearts of men. In all His teaching about life and conduct He avoids the trifling and the superficial. He almost ignores mere outward doings, and goes down to the secret springs of thought, desire, and motive.

9. The teaching of Jesus carries with it a peculiar impression of *authority* (see Mark i. 22). The words of this Galilean peasant seemed to His hearers then, and seem to us who read them now, absolutely trustworthy and intrinsically true, needing no confirmation beyond that of His character and personality.

10. There was about Jesus an extraordinary *breadth of sympathy and interest*. He belonged to one of the narrowest of peoples, the Jews, but He was absolutely free from all their national prejudices and peculiarities. To-day His teaching comes as appropriately to the Hindoo or the Laplander as to the Englishman. Jesus lived at a particular time in history, and yet there are about Him none of the special features of any particular period. His character remains as beautiful and as perfect for the twentieth century as it was for the first. He delighted to

call Himself *the Son of Man,* and, whatever that much-discussed phrase may mean, it certainly means this among other things: that He belongs, not to any one family or race, but to all men ; and, not to any one age, but to all time.

11. The Evangelists are continually pointing out a unique connexion between Jesus and the past. As they put it, *prophecy was fulfilled in Him.* Some of the passages they quote are less convincing than others, as they were written in the first instance with reference to some one other than Christ. But many of them are, to say the least, surprisingly appropriate when applied to Christ. Much more striking, however, is the way in which Jesus *fulfils or completes the Old Testament system as a whole.*

(1) By adding the doctrine of the Fatherhood He put the finishing touch to the noble conception of God found in the highest parts of the Old Testament.

(2) He fulfilled, with wonderful completeness and accuracy, the long hope and desire for the Messiah expressed in the Prophets, although He was very different in His life and work from the expectations which the Jews had formed.

(3) He perfected the Old Testament morality by re-interpreting the Ten Commandments, and by His new commandment of love.

(4) He carried Religion forward the last stage by making it purely spiritual, and no longer dependent on either ceremonies or sacrifices. Only after His death, however, did His disciples realize that He Himself was the last great Sacrifice, which made all other sacrifices henceforth superfluous.

It will thus be seen that the Character, Teaching and Death of Jesus dovetail into the Old Testament system of religion and doctrine, and make it perfect and complete.

D.—THE DIVINITY OF CHRIST

Great as the claims are that have been made for Jesus in this chapter, we have had no proof, as yet, that He was divine.   Sinlessness and miraculous power are what we should expect if He was divine, but they do not, in themselves, *prove* His Divinity.   A man might be so endowed with the Spirit of God as to be sinless in life and superhuman in power, and yet be only a Spirit-filled *man*.   If there were nothing more to urge, it would suffice to describe Jesus as the holiest of men, or the greatest of the Prophets ; or, we might accept one of the many theories according to which He was semi-divine, a created Being, greater than man but less than God.

We may include under the name of *Unitarianism* a great variety of beliefs which deny the real Divinity of Christ, some of them approaching the Christian view so nearly as to be almost indistinguishable from it.   But they will all be found to part company with the Christian belief at one or other of the following points:

1.   Christianity claims that Jesus differed from men in *kind,* not merely in *degree ;* and it accordingly denies that men are " potential Christs " or " Christs in the making."

2.   It claims that Jesus is the *only* Son of God, in the full sense of the words, and that His Sonship is of a different order from that into which men may enter by faith.

3.   It claims that Jesus is the *eternal* Son of God, uncreated and without beginning in Time.

4.   It claims that Jesus is *one with God,* with a Divine Nature different from the " spark of the Divine " which exists in men.

These four statements together define what we mean by the Divinity of Christ.

They are extraordinary claims to make, and it is difficult to say what would constitute an absolutely conclusive proof of them.   Supposing that God actually appeared among men, by what sort of evidence could He satisfy all men and all ages that He had done so?   Our reason for accepting the Divinity of Christ is that there are four facts, which no other theory of His Person can account for, but which are satisfactorily explained by the Christian doctrine. The facts are these:

1. The claims which Jesus made for Himself.

2. The convictions of His first disciples concerning Him.

3. The personal experience of multitudes of believers.

4. The influence of Christianity in History.

1. *The Claims of Jesus for Himself*

Jesus consistently avoided all self-aggrandizement, and refused the honours that men, at times, sought to thrust upon Him. His whole history is that of One who was "meek and lowly in heart." Yet He made claims for Himself so stupendous that in the case of any other man they would be regarded as blasphemy or madness. Many since His day have claimed to be the Messiah, but their claims have excited only horror or derision. True, the priestly party in His own day accused Jesus of blasphemy; but it is patent to every reader of the Gospels that, whatever Jesus was, His enemies completely misjudged Him. It is simply unthinkable that He was a conscious blasphemer; and it is equally impossible to regard Him as a fanatic or a madman.

Modern unbelief frequently adopts the one alternative that remains, and asserts that in these sayings we have, not genuine words of Jesus, but utterances that extravagant and enthusiastic disciples attributed to Him in later days. If there were any truth in this suggestion it would be most likely to apply to the Gospel according to St. John. Few, however, will question the general reliability of the *three Synoptic Gospels;* and confining ourselves, for the present, to these, we shall find many sayings of Jesus in which the most exalted claims are either expressed or implied. Some of those in which the claim is implied incidentally, when He is not speaking directly of His own Person or Work, are specially impressive; for in these we get, so to speak, an accidental and unintentional disclosure of His thoughts about Himself.

It is often said that in the Sermon on the Mount we have a " simple human Jesus," and that this is the real Jesus, But is it a merely human Jesus who dares to supersede the teaching of the Old Testament with His bold " *I* say unto you "?   Note that He makes no attempt to prove His title to such authority ; He takes it for granted.

And what is to be said of such a passage as this?

" Many will say to Me in that day, Lord, Lord, did we not prophesy by Thy name, and by Thy name cast out devils, and by Thy name do many mighty works ? And then will I profess unto them, I never knew you : depart from Me, ye that work iniquity " (Matt. vii. 22, 23).

We have far more than a simple human Jesus here!
Passing from the Sermon on the Mount, we may select the following as a few out of many sayings that deserve consideration:

" The Son of Man is Lord of the Sabbath " (Luke vi. 5).

" Come unto Me, all ye that labour and are heavy laden, and I will give you rest " (Matt. xi. 28).

" The Son of man hath power on earth to forgive sins " (Mark ii. 10).

" Whosoever shall lose his life for My sake and the Gospel's shall save it " (Mark viii. 35).

" He that denieth Me in the presence of men shall be denied in the presence of the angels of God " (Luke xii. 9).

" If any man cometh unto Me, and hateth not his own father, . . . yea, and his own life also, he cannot be My disciple " (Luke xiv. 26).

" This is My blood of the covenant, which is shed for many unto remission of sins " (Matt. xxvi. 28).

" Again the high priest asked Him, and saith unto Him Art Thou the Christ, the Son of the Blessed ? And Jesus said, I am : and ye shall see the Son of man sitting at the right hand of power, and coming with the clouds of heaven " (Mark xiv. 61, 62).

The Synoptic Gospels also tell us that He accepted Peter's description of Him as the Son of God (Matt. xvi. 16), that He pronounced words of forgiveness (Luke v. 20, vii. 48), and that He allowed men to pray to him

(Matt. xvii. 14 ; Luke xvii. 5). They also show us that, whilst He taught His disciples to pray together, He Himself prayed apart. It is notable, too, that He spoke of God as " *My* Father " or " *Your* Father," never as " *Our* Father," except in the Lord's Prayer, which He gave to the disciples for use amongst themselves, and not in conjunction with Himself.

No claims could go further, and, in the light of these quotations from the Synoptics, there is no difficulty in accepting as genuine similar sayings recorded in the *Fourth Gospel.* The following quotations from John should therefore be noted:

" I am the light of the world " (viii. 12).

" I am the way, and the truth, and the life " (xiv. 6).

" Before Abraham was, I am " (viii. 58).

" He that hath seen Me, hath seen the Father " (xiv. 9).

" I and the Father are one " (x. 30).

Unless we are to suppose that we can know nothing reliable concerning Jesus, it is, therefore, certain that He Himself distinctly claimed Divine origin, Divine powers, and Divine authority. These claims are made deliberately, soberly, and repeatedly ; and they are also implied continually in almost every utterance of His. We cannot refuse to believe what a man of proved integrity and worth may tell us concerning himself, merely on the ground that it is his own testimony. These stupendous claims of Jesus are borne out by His whole character and work. The loftiest and serenest Being this world has known was neither blasphemer nor fanatic. We are bound to accept His claims as true.

2. *The Belief of the Disciples*

Our next reason for accepting the Divinity of Christ is that it was an intense and passionate conviction with those who lived nearest to Him and knew Him most intimately. Even if the testimony of Jesus to Himself could be explained away or dismissed as of no account, we should still have to meet the testimony of His disciples.

C

The more we consider their witness, the greater is the impression it produces.

(1) It is hardly possible to imagine witnesses more difficult to convince or less likely to be deceived. Let us try to imagine the obstacles to belief in their case. (a) They were *Jews,* and this implies that woven into the very fibre of their being was the belief that God is One. Though it required centuries of teaching and a succession of national calamities to make them learn it, the Jews had learnt that lesson for all time. Yet these Jewish disciples came to believe that Jesus was one with God. (b) Many of them were *relatives and friends,* who had known Him intimately and had seen whatever of mortal weakness His human life could show ; and for them belief must have been correspondingly difficult. Yet His mother, who had nursed Him as a helpless babe ; His brethren, who had known Him as a child, a school-boy, an apprentice, and an artisan ; the Eleven, who had seen Him weary and sorrowful: all these came to believe that He was God Incarnate. (c) Some of the witnesses had been *bitter and scornful foes,* like Saul of Tarsus. Yet they too accepted the belief with passionate enthusiasm. (d) Most of them had seen Him die, and *die by crucifixion.* Whatever roll of shame there may have been corresponding to the New-gate Calendar of our day, they all knew that His name was written there. And yet they believed!

(2) Their testimony was *absolutely unanimous.* Such a conviction cannot have resulted from the fanaticism of a few, for after the Resurrection we hear of not a single dissentient: even doubting Thomas joined with the rest in hailing Christ as Lord and God. The New Testament is saturated with this belief ; but the following passages selected from the different sections of the New Testament will suffice to show how unanimous His followers were, and they should be carefully studied: Rom. i. 4 ; Gal. iv. 4 ; Phil. ii. 6, 7 ; Heb. i. 1 - 4 ; James ii. 1 ; 1 Peter iv. 11 ; John i. 14 ; 1 John iv. 15 ; Rev. i. 5 - 7.

(3) That the disciples were not fanatical enthusiasts is shown by the attempts that they made to construct a

reasoned explanation of the mystery. The Epistles to the Romans, the Ephesians, and the Hebrews, all have the meaning and purpose of the Incarnation for their main theme.

(4) The book of the Acts makes it abundantly clear that the disciples showed the reality of their belief by a *consistent attitude towards Christ* in their daily life and their missionary work. They prayed to Him, they claimed that their miracles were wrought by His power, they preached salvation in His Name, and they looked forward to His return in glory to judge the world.

(5) It must be noted that these witnesses were *utterly disinterested and sincere*. So far as this world was concerned, the disciples had everything to lose and nothing to gain by proclaiming this belief. For every one of them it meant ridicule and persecution ; for some, like St. Paul, it involved the loss of fortune and of friends, and the sacrifice of all their prospects in life ; for many it implied missionary work of almost incredible toil and hardship ; and in the case of large numbers of them it resulted in the agonizing death of the martyr.

Yet they were men to whom this mystery must have seemed even more difficult of belief than it does to us. We can only conclude that it must have been an overwhelming evidence which produced a conviction so intense, and a testimony so unanimous, consistent, and heroic.

3. *The Experience of Believers to-day*

The testimony to the Divinity of our Lord increases in volume year by year. Each new generation has been marked by a growth of the Christian Church, both in numbers and in influence, until to-day we have a " great cloud of witnesses."

(1) We may consider, first, *the character of our modern witnesses*. There are two important points to be noticed: (*a*) We find amongst the witnesses men and women of *all types and all temperaments*. In our own land the Church includes in its membership men of ancient family

and noble rank : men of weight in the councils of the state ; men of eminence in all departments of learning, literature, art, science, and medicine ; men of fame in war ; and a number of the great captains of industry and princes of our commerce. Any man you pass in the street, schoolmaster or mechanic, clerk or ploughman, invalid or athlete, may prove to be an earnest and humble believer. Though it is sometimes said that Christianity has lost its hold upon the masses, the majority of the representatives of Labour in our Parliament are active members of the Church. Surely there must be truth in a belief which has been held with equal tenacity by Queens and working girls, and by Prime Ministers and labouring men.

(b) The witnesses include men and women from *every nation* under heaven. They may be found in Western Europe and in Central Africa, in the Frozen North and in the islands of the Sea, "a great multitude which no man could number, out of every nation, and of all tribes and peoples and tongues" (Rev. vii. 9). Our belief must represent some fundamental truth, for it finds a response in every section of the human race.

(2) Let us now examine *the testimony borne* by these modern witnesses. Here again there are two points to be noted: (a) They all admit that their conviction is a matter of *faith,* not of knowledge ; but they all assert that it is *not incredible.* The mystery is there, and "we have but faith, we cannot know"; yet the difficulties of belief are not insuperable, and the most intellectual of men may hold the Faith without doing violence to his reason.

(b) The witnesses also agree in testifying that *this belief can work a change in the life.* Not merely do they believe in a Divine Christ, but they assert that they have found Him in *their own experience.* Some have been drawn up out of the miry clay ; some have passed "from darkness to light"; and for others all things have become new. Through this belief many have passed away in glorious triumph over death and its terrors. Old saints are waiting for the end in happy expectation ; many have found a peace "which passeth all understanding"; and others are fighting manfully the battle of life—all as the outcome of this belief. Those who call it a delusion have to account for such results.

4. *The Influence of Christianity in History*

There remains one further reason for believing in this foundation doctrine of the Christian Faith, namely, that Christianity has been the mightiest of all influences for good in the history of mankind.

(1) It is a very remarkable fact that during the last nineteen hundred years *the progressive nations of the world have been the Christian nations*. Whatever advance has been made in knowledge, in industries and commerce, in art and medicine, and in the betterment of social conditions, has been confined almost exclusively to the Christian nations. The one apparent exception is the case of Japan. But, admittedly, Japan has borrowed its civilization from the Christian West ; and it still remains to be seen how long she will be able to maintain her position, if she declines to accept the Christian Religion.

(2) It is undeniable that *national life has reached its highest level in the Christian nations,* for Christianity has continually tended to promote *Peace, Justice,* and *Liberty.* (*a*) We cannot deny that the history of Europe for the last thirty years has been one of terrible wars and rumours of wars. But it is also true that all Christian men deplore it, and feel increasingly that war is a horrible and barbarous method of settling disputes. All Christian sentiment is behind such peace ideals as are represented by the League of Nations, and war deeply troubles the *conscience* of Christian men quite apart from all the terrible suffering and loss that it may bring. In pre-Christian civilizations war might be hated and feared, but it was not felt to be wicked and unworthy of good men. It is only in so far as men or nations have *abandoned* Christianity that they can be brought in a land like this to acquiesce in any war, except one of defence of our own land or of smaller peoples. Some question whether even such a war as that can ever be right. (*b*) As regards

Justice, it is doubtful whether it can be found at all outside the sphere of Christian influence. In most Eastern lands the native courts are still courts of injustice, where the verdict can be won only by bribing both the witnesses and the judge. (*c*) A moment's comparison of the position of the subject in Britain with his position in such a country as Persia will show how much has been done in Christian lands to secure the *liberty* of the individual. It is not merely that Christianity abolished slavery: it has produced nearly all our most precious personal rights, such as freedom of thought, freedom of speech and freedom of the Press. As regards Russia, it must be remembered that the servile condition of the peasants before the revolution there was largely due to the deadness and formality of the Greek Church; and the absence of personal liberty in modern Russia is mainly a consequence of State atheism. Similarly, in present-day Germany the destruction of personal freedom has only become possible by the substitution of a bastard Christianity and an " Aryan God " for the God and Father of our Lord Jesus Christ; hence the bitter conflict there between Church and State. To see the natural outcome of the Christian belief about man as a living soul and a child of God working itself out freely we must look at Britain, the Scandinavian nations and the United States; and there we find neither slavery nor serfdom nor the pitiless subjection of the individual to the State, but representative government and respect for all the rights of the individual.

(3) What we know as a *Home* does not exist apart from Christianity. In non-Christian lands woman is still an inferior and a toy, even when she is treated with indulgence. Infant girls are still exposed to die in China, and child-wives of tender years are common in India.

(4) A vast multitude of *charitable and philanthropic enterprises*, such as hospitals, almshouses and orphan homes, owe their origin to Christianity. They did not exist in a great and wealthy city like ancient Rome; and, apart from Christian influence and example, they do not exist in non-Christian lands to-day. This is not to claim that it is only the avowedly Christian portion of the com-

munity that is responsible for the charitable work of our day. But the Christian Church is still foremost in such enterprises, and that noble spirit of philanthropy which is often found in England to-day outside the Churches is itself the result of Christian teaching and example. The beautiful characters of many who do not profess the Faith may be compared to cut blooms detached from their roots, for they had their origin in early Christian training or in a godly ancestry.

(5) Perhaps the most distinctive outcome of the Christian Faith is that *interest in the lost, the fallen, and the degraded,* which inspires our great missionary enterprises at home and abroad. The doctrine of the Incarnation gives a new value to human nature, and compels us to believe both that the worst are worth saving and that they can be saved. The extraordinary success of such work, especially amongst the most degraded heathen races and in the slums of our great towns, is a striking evidence of the truth of the Faith on which the Christian message is based.

CONCLUSION

We may now proceed to sum up our case.

(1) *There is no objection that can be urged,* except that the doctrine implies a stupendous miracle.

(2) *All the evidence is in its favour:* the life and character of Jesus, the words of Jesus, the conviction of His disciples, the experience of believers to-day, and the influence of Christianity for good —all bear the same testimony.

(3) *There is no witness missing* who might perhaps testify against it ; that is, it cannot be said that any important evidence has been lost.

(4) *The Faith has survived for nineteen hundred years,* in spite of ruthless persecution and bitter critical attacks, and in spite of the unworthiness, the dissensions, and the follies of the Christian Church.

E.—THE HUMANITY OF OUR LORD

Whilst we maintain the real Divinity of our Lord, we must be careful to do justice to His Humanity also. In earlier days attempts were made to escape the perplexities of the doctrine of the Incarnation by denying the real Humanity of Jesus. Several theories were put forward, the simplest being that His body was a mere appearance or phantom. This view is called *Docetism,* from the Greek word meaning " to seem." Protests against such a theory are found in the New Testament itself, e.g., in 1 John i. 1, 2, and in other passages such as these:

" The Word became *flesh* " (John 1. 14).

" Every spirit which confesseth that Jesus Christ is come in the *flesh* is of God " (1 John iv. 2).

" One mediator also between God and men, Himself *man,* Christ Jesus " (1 Tim. ii. 5).

The Gospel narrative is the story of a really human life, lived in a human *body:* Jesus was born, He grew, He hungered, He thirsted, He was wearied, He died, and His body was laid in the tomb. His *mind* had also the essential human characteristics: He had to learn, for He " increased in wisdom " (Luke ii. 52) ; He had sometimes to ask questions on matters of ordinary fact, e.g., " Who touched My garments? " (Mark v. 30), and " How long time is it since this hath come unto him?" (Mark ix. 21) ; and, further, He sometimes felt suprise, e.g., " And when Jesus heard these things, He marvelled at him " (Luke vii. 9). He had the ordinary human *feelings* and *affections:* He loved, He was grieved, He was indignant, He wept. Even in the life of the *spirit* He was subject to human conditions: He could be tempted, really and sorely tempted (see Luke iv. 2 ; John xii. 27, 28 ; Luke xxii. 28 ; Matt. xxvi. 38, 39), and He was dependent on prayer.

F.—GOD AND MAN

The most difficult of all theological problems is to form a satisfactory theory of the Incarnation, or doctrine of the Person of Christ.

Any true theory must do full justice to both the real

Divinity and the full Humanity of our Lord. Jesus Christ was not God only, nor man only ; nor an intermediate being, neither God nor man ; but God *and* man. Yet the two natures were perfectly united: He was only one Person, with one mind and one will, for there is no trace of any division in His life like the distinction between the official character and the private character of an earthly dignitary.

So long as we conceive of God only as the Absolute and the Eternal, infinitely remote from man, such a union of God and man is unthinkable ; we could as easily imagine a union between a star and a fly. But long before we read of the Incarnation, the Bible teaches us that God is a Person, with thought, will, and love, and that there is a real kinship between Him and man, since man is made in His image. That is to say, there is something corresponding with humanity in God, and something corresponding with divinity in man, so that a union of the two is not inconceivable.

The word *Incarnation* means a becoming flesh or entering into flesh, and was suggested by the statement that " the Word became flesh " (John i. 14). Why was Jesus Christ described as *the Word* or *Logos* ? A thought is a spiritual thing, invisible and inaudible ; a sound is a material thing, a movement of air ; but a *word* is a combination of the two, a thought become audible, so that it is spiritual and material at the same time. A word is a thought embodied in a material form. Jesus Christ was the Word of God, that is, the mind and will and love of God uttered forth in a material form by His becoming flesh. He was God's expression of Himself in a human life.

Electricity is an invisible force, diffused throughout the Universe ; and the carbons in an electric arc-lamp are pieces of black charcoal. But through the medium of the carbons the electricity renders itself visible in the form of light, and the black carbons are transformed to a dazzling whiteness. In Jesus Christ the infinite and invisible God made Himself visible through union with a human life, whilst at the same time Humanity appeared transfigured in the person of the Ideal Man.

In the statement that Christ "emptied Himself" (Phil. ii. 7), St. Paul describes the change that took place in Him when He became man. It was an act of infinite condescension and humiliation. There was more in God than human nature could hold, and our Lord could only become man by emptying Himself, so far as His Incarnation was concerned, of much that was peculiarly divine. It is clear that He surrendered His omnipresence ; and, marvellous as His powers were, they hardly amounted here to omnipotence. He surrendered His glory, though for a moment it shone forth again at the Transfiguration.

What was the effect upon His knowledge of this self-emptying or *Kenosis,* as it is called? It is clear from the Gospels that, though He had a wonderful insight into the hearts of men (see John i. 47 - 49 and ii. 25), His knowledge of matters of ordinary fact was very similar to that of other men. Even in spiritual matters He admitted that He did not know the day or the hour of the End (Mark xiii. 32). Yet the very terms He used on that occasion, "not even the angels in heaven, neither the Son," were virtually a claim to complete knowledge of other spiritual things ; so that this one reservation does not prevent us from admitting His claim to be the Light of the World.

Just as a portrait is all that can be shown of a man in oils and canvas, so Jesus is the portrait of God, all that could be shown of God under the conditions of mortal flesh ; and He had the right to say, "He that hath seen Me hath seen the Father" (John xiv. 9). Compare with this the striking description of Jesus in Hebrews i. 3, "the effulgence of His (i.e., God's) glory, and the very image of His substance."

CHAPTER V

Jesus Christ the Saviour of Men

WE come now to consider the purpose of the Incarnation. In the belief of the Christian Church the purpose that led up to it was not unworthy of even so stupendous an event. The question, *Why did the Son of God become man ?* may be answered in the familiar words of the Nicene Creed: "Who for us men and for our salvation came down from heaven, and was incarnate by the Holy Ghost of the Virgin Mary."

Even before His Birth this purpose of Salvation was indicated in His name of "Jesus," which meant Saviour (see Matt. i. 21) ; and it is re-affirmed in the words of Christ Himself, "The Son of man came to seek and to save that which was lost" (Luke xix. 10), and also in the words of St. Paul, "Christ Jesus came into the world to save sinners" (1 Tim. i. 15).

Whilst His Death was unquestionably the supreme factor in Christ's saving Work, all that He was and did also contributed towards it ; and in some respects His work is not finished even now. The phrases, "The *beginning* of the Gospel" (Mark i. 1), and "all that Jesus *began* both to do and to teach" (Acts i. 1), both indicate that our Lord's earthly Ministry and Death were regarded as only the beginning of His Work.

A.—HIS INCARNATION AND BIRTH

The mere fact that Christ was born into the world in itself did something towards our salvation.

1. *He brought God near to us.* Men, who were separated from God, by reason of their earthly nature and even more by reason of their sin, needed One who could

serve as a link between them and God ; and the ideal link was found in Jesus Christ, the Mediator, who is both God and man. The doctrine of the Virgin Birth, according to which He " was conceived by the Holy Ghost, born of the Virgin Mary," enables us to understand how He could be at once human and divine.

2. *The Birth of Jesus gave a new beginning to the Race,* and He is therefore called " the last Adam " or " the second man " (1 Cor. xv. 45, 47). It may almost be said that the Race was born again in Him. The title " the Son of man," which He so often used, means, not the Son of *a* man, but rather the Son of Mankind ; and it suggests a peculiar relationship to the whole Race. And just as the first Adam is described in Genesis as the direct creation of God, so, according to the doctrine of the Virgin Birth, the second Adam came into the world through the action of the Spirit, God's great Agent in creation.

3. Whilst we are not " Christs in the making," and can never become all that He was, yet the fact that the Son of God lived the life of a man has set up *a higher and more spiritual ideal* of what man may be. Here again the doctrine of the Virgin Birth is significant, for it indicates a way in which Jesus might be the *Ideal Man,* truly human but without that taint of sin which a normal birth would have involved.

B.—HIS REVELATION OF GOD

Jesus gave the world an enlarged and purified conception of God, in which both God and His service are presented so attractively that men have been drawn by it into the right way.

Christ is rightly called the *Word of God,* for He has declared God as no other could. But that term reminds us that He was more than God's *messenger,* He was Himself God's *message ;* for we learn what God is like, quite as much from what Jesus *did* and *was,* as from what He *said.*

1. The most novel and attractive points in the *teaching of Jesus concerning God* are these: (*a*) His doctrine of God's Fatherhood and Love ; (*b*) The stress He laid on

the spirituality of God, and the consequent need of inward purity and sincerity in His service ; (c) The place He gave to love as man's chief duty towards God ; (d) His declaration that God longs to recover His lost and rebellious children.

2. Jesus claimed that those who had seen Him had seen the Father (see John xiv. 9). This means that *His life and character* were meant to show men *a living portrait of God*. If this be so, we have the right to include in our conception of God every noble and gracious quality that we see in the character of Jesus. It is one of the ironies of the religious life that many love Jesus but feel a certain dread of God ; for whatever was lovable in Jesus exists fundamentally in the Father, whose portrait He was. If we can believe that God is like Jesus, we can ascribe to Him: (a) Almighty power ; (b) A tender pity for men in their sufferings and sorrows ; (c) A great hatred of sin ; (d) A love that will not let the sinner go ; (e) A great willingness to forgive.

C.—HIS MORAL TEACHING AND EXAMPLE

Jesus further assisted towards the salvation of men by setting before them a new ideal of life and conduct and showing them what *goodness* means.

1. *His Teaching*. There are few who do not recognize that in such *moral teaching* as the Sermon on the Mount we have a sublime conception of what human life may be, an ideal which, even when men fail to attain it, ennobles them in the attempt. The most important elements in this ideal are : (a) A simple and childlike dependence upon God ; (b) Love towards God casting out fear ; (c) Genuineness and sincerity in all the relationships of life ; (d) Love as our chief duty towards our fellows ; (e) The absolute superiority of the claims of the spiritual life above those of the material.

2. *His example*. It is often harder to practise than to preach. Jesus, however, did both ; and even more important than His moral teaching is His *example*. (1) His

example illustrates His teaching, and sometimes throws light on sayings that in themselves are perplexing, such as some of the precepts in the Sermon on the Mount. (2) His example is an everlasting proof that the ideal He set before men is a practicable one: the sinless life of love is possible, for it has been lived. (3) Jesus had a very full and varied experience of life, especially of those things which most try men: poverty, hardship, laborious work, ingratitude, misunderstanding, unmerited reproach, and hatred. He was tempted, and He had to face man's last great enemy, Death. So that, whilst our lives are necessarily very different from His in their routine, there are hardly any circumstances conceivable in which we may not find both guidance and encouragement in His example.

D.—THE ATONING DEATH OF CHRIST

Unquestionably, according to the teaching of Scripture, our Lord's supreme work for the salvation of men was accomplished in His Death: all that He has done and is doing for us culminated in the Cross and is focused there in Christian thought.

The word *Atonement* is used to describe this work. We almost inevitably think of it as meaning a propitiatory offering. Yet it was originally spelt *at-one-ment*, and so meant reconciliation. The object of Christ's Death was to effect a reconciliation between men and God ; but the name Atonement is now generally given, not to that reconciliation, but to *the means used* to effect it, namely, Christ's sacrificial Death.

It is sometimes said that this doctrine does not belong to the original teaching of Christianity, and that we owe it to the genius of St. Paul and not to the teaching of Christ. The facts, however, are as follows:

1. The doctrine is found in germ in the *words of Jesus* Himself, e.g.:

" From that time began Jesus to show unto His disciples, how that He *must* go unto Jerusalem . . . and be killed " (Matt. xvi. 21).

" For verily the Son of man came not to be ministered unto, but to minister, and to *give His life* a ransom for many " (Mark x. 45).

" This is My blood of the Covenant, which is *shed for many* unto remission of sins " (Matt. xxvi. 28).

2.   The doctrine is also found in *the earliest preaching* recorded in the Acts, though it certainly figures less prominently than the Resurrection.   The fact is that for some time the disciples were sorely perplexed by the shameful Death of Christ.   They understood readily enough the wonder of the Resurrection and much of what it implied as to the dignity of their Lord ; and the result was that, at first, the Resurrection formed their principal theme. But, though they hardly understood as yet the reason for its necessity, the earliest Christian preachers recognized that the Death of Christ was strictly necessary, and that it formed *part of the Divine plan*.   For instance, in the earliest sermon of all St. Peter speaks of Christ as " delivered up by the determinate counsel and foreknowledge of God " (Acts ii. 23).

3.   The rest of the Acts and the Epistles as a whole afford ample evidence that the belief in the Atonement was *perfectly familiar* in all the Christian Churches.   But the mystery was so profound that it was not until after the giant intellect of St. Paul, aided by the Holy Spirit, had wrestled with the problem for some years that it became possible to set forth a reasoned explanation of it.   What Christianity owes to St. Paul is not the doctrine of the Atonement, but the *theory* of it: he did not create the doctrine, he explained it.

The Doctrine of the Atonement

1.   *Man's Guilt and Helplessness.*   Any exposition of the Atonement must start from the facts that men have sinned and that sin involves guilt and separation from God.   Yet there is no way in which men can undo the past, and no reparation that they can make to God.   Whatever a man may give to God, even though it be his firstborn, was itself God's gift to him.   Whatever a man may do that is noble or holy, is done by means of powers which

God first bestowed upon him. There is nothing that we can offer to God, or be or do for His sake, that is not already His. We may go beyond our duty to men, we may pay them more than we owe, and we may do for them more than they have any just right to expect of us. But we can never do more than our duty to God, and we can never make Him our debtor. As our Maker He has a natural claim to *all* that we can do and the *best* that we can do ; so that we can never acquire any surplus of merit, which might avail to cancel the sin of the past ; for, as Tennyson puts it:

> merit lives from man to man,
> And not from man, O Lord, to Thee.

The holiest of men in his holiest day can do no more than that day's duty: when we have done all, we are still non-profitable servants (see Luke xvii. 10), for we cannot enrich God by rendering back to Him more than He first put within us.

2. *God's Longing to forgive Men.* A second point of vital importance is that God in His love longs to forgive men and to be at peace with them. The Atonement is emphatically *not* an appeasement of an angry God, whereby He is induced to forgive us. God is, indeed, "angry with the wicked," in the sense that His wrath burns against their sin, and against them in so far as they identify themselves with their sin. But, considered apart from their sin, God loves the worst of men with an infinite love, and longs to forgive them. *The Atonement originated in the heart of God ;* and, if other religions show us men giving their best to God, Christianity shows us God giving His best to and for men: "*God* so loved the world that He gave His only begotten Son" (John iii. 16). Cf. also, "God commendeth *His own love* towards us, in that, while we were yet sinners, Christ died for us" (Rom. v. 8). If the Atonement was an act of reconciliation, it was rebellious men, and not God, who needed to be reconciled, for "God was in Christ reconciling the world *unto Himself*" (2 Cor. v. 19).

3. *The need of an Atonement.* It may be asked, how-

ever, if God longs to forgive men, why should any atonement be necessary? Why does He not forgive as an earthly father forgives, without any question of compensation or reparation? It must not be thought that the Atonement was an offering made for the tender-hearted Son to appease an angry God. In so far as our sins may be wrongs done to God personally, He does freely and absolutely forgive them, and the Atonement is not a compensation offered to Him for injuries that men have done to Him. But there is another aspect to our sins: they are offences against the eternal Law of Right, that Law which God not only imposes upon men, but by which He also consents to be bound Himself. We generally identify this Law with the Will of God, but it is possible to separate the two in thought. And, though God might forgive without atonement our offences against Himself, as a holy God He cannot ignore the claims of violated Law. If He did so, He would Himself be unjust in the very act of forgiving and justifying men. The father who forgives his child a theft from a neighbour without any attempt to make reparation, or who forgives him a lie without any attempt to enforce the claims of truth, is himself acquiescing in and condoning the theft or the lie. The Atonement was necessary, not to *induce* God to forgive, but to *enable* Him to forgive sin without injustice. If the classical passage, Rom. iii. 21 - 26, is carefully studied, it will be seen that the Atonement was not an offering made to satisfy any sense of injury in God, but *God's offering,* in the person of His Son, to satisfy the claims of Righteousness.

4. *Christ's Fitness to make the Atonement.* There were four qualifications, belonging to Christ alone, which fitted Him to atone for the sin of the whole world. (1) He was *divine,* and, as the Son of God, His merits are literally of infinite and immeasurable worth, sufficient to avail for the whole race. (2) He was *human,* and, as the Son of man, He was fitted to stand as the representative of the whole human family. (3) He was *sinless,* and therefore able to do that which was impossible to sin-stained men. (4) He was *eternal.* If the common translation of Rev. xiii. 8, " the Lamb that hath been slain from the foundation of the world," is correct, both that passage

and Heb. ix. 14, indicate that though Christ's Sacrifice occurred at an actual date in history, yet in the eternal mind both of the Father and of the Son, is was accomplished from all eternity. This enables us to understand how its atoning merit reaches back to meet the need of all men from the beginning, and also reaches forward to meet the need of those who are yet to be born.

5. *The connexion between Death and Atonement.* The question now arises: Admitting that Christ made an atonement for sin, why should we regard it as accomplished in His *Death* rather than by His Life of Sacrifice? was it essential that He should *die?* The work of atonement was perhaps not confined solely to the tragedy on Calvary, for the spirit that brought Christ to Calvary animated His whole life, and the shadow of the Cross fell upon Him at a comparatively early stage. Yet it is true that His redeeming work was concentrated in the Death upon the Cross.

It must be remembered that the Bible regards *death* as the peculiar consequence and penalty of *sin* (see Ezek. xviii. 4 ; Rom. v. 12). Even on the Evolutionary Theory it is by no means clear that the first man was necessarily mortal: in the original purpose of God he might have been immortal, or the end of physical life might have come in some such way as is recorded of Enoch. The end might have been a painless and happy transformation, like that of the chrysalis when it becomes a butterfly: cf. the language St. Paul uses in 1 Cor. xv. 52 and 1 Thess. iv. 17, of the change to be experienced by those who survive until the Second Coming. At any rate, according to the Bible, "the *sting* of death is sin" (1 Cor. xv. 56), that is, death has become the dark and dreadful experience that it is to men because of sin.

Hence it was fitting that in atoning for sin Christ should die, for death represents the consequences and penalties of sin. This is the point of the words, "Apart from shedding of blood there is no remission" (Heb. ix. 22). This aspect of the Death of Christ becomes still more prominent when we remember that He died the kind of death reserved by the Roman law for the *punishment of criminals*.

Moreover, it was this element in His Death which was the cause of the agony of Gethsemane and of Calvary. The mere physical *pain* was of little moment, and even the fact that He died *through* the sin of men, in consequence of the malice and hatred of men, was of little moment in comparison with the *spiritual shame and anguish* of taking upon Himself the sin and guilt for which death stood. It is believed by some that Jesus died, not as the direct result of crucifixion, but from a broken heart, caused by the fact that in dying He became the representative of the sin and guilt of men, or, to use the awful words of St. Paul, He was " made to be sin " on our behalf (2 Cor. v. 21). This also accounts for His terrible experience of desertion by the Father, for sin always separates from God. Christ *tasted* death as no other has done, He drained the cup of bitterness to the last drop, and realized in its fulness all that death means.

The general theory of the Atonement may, therefore, be stated thus:

By yielding Himself to death at the hands of men, and dying the death of a criminal, Christ, as our Representative and for our sakes, took upon Himself the peculiar consequences of Sin. He thus satisfied the claims of Righteousness, and made it possible for God to fulfil His loving desire to forgive sinful men without violating the principle of Right.

6. *Various ways of stating the Atonement in Scripture.* A mystery so great as the Atonement has necessarily many aspects, and may be regarded from many points of view and stated in many different ways. Considerations of space forbid any detailed exposition of the notable statements of the New Testament on the subject, but the following selection of passages will show how many different elements enter into any complete view of the doctrine. It will be noticed that the language is almost always figurative ; and it should be borne in mind that,

since few analogies are true at more than one or two points, it is unsafe to press any one of them without due reference to others.

(1) Salvation through Christ's *obedience* :

" For as through the one man's disobedience the many were made sinners, even so through the obedience of the one shall the many be made righteous " (Rom. v. 19).

" Becoming obedient even unto death, yea, the death of the cross " (Phil. ii. 8).

The meaning of the latter passage is, of course, that Christ obeyed the Father to the last possible point, even to the extreme of dying.

(2) Christ's Death the payment of our *ransom* or *redemption* price:

" For verily the Son of man came not to be ministered unto, but to minister, and to give His life a ransom for many " (Mark x. 45).

" In Whom we have our redemption through His blood " (Eph. i. 7).

" Ye were redeemed not with corruptible things, with silver or gold . . . but with precious blood . . . even the blood of Christ " (1 Pet. i. 18, 19).

Questions have been raised as to who received the price. Some have actually suggested the devil! Christ's Death was a moral equivalent or price paid to the Law of Righteousness, or to the Order of the Universe.

(3) Christ as our *sacrifice,* making *propitiation* for us:

" For our passover also hath been sacrificed, even Christ " (1 Cor. v. 7).

" Behold, the Lamb of God, which taketh away the sin of the world " (John i. 29).

" For if the blood of goats and bulls, and the ashes of a heifer, sprinkling them that have been defiled, sanctify unto the cleanness of the flesh : how much more shall the blood of Christ, who through the eternal Spirit offered Himself without blemish unto God, cleanse your conscience from dead works to serve the living God " (Heb. ix. 13, 14).

" He, when He had offered one sacrifice for sins for ever, sat down on the right hand of God " (Heb. x. 12).

" He is the propitiation for our sins ; and not for ours only, but also for the whole world " (1 John ii. 2).

(4) Christ's Death an act of *reconciliation :*

" God was in Christ reconciling the world unto Himself, not reckoning unto them their trespass " (2 Cor. v. 19).

(5) Christ bearing our *curse* or condemnation:

" Christ redeemed us from the curse of the law, having become a curse for us : for it is written, Cursed is every one that hangeth on a tree " (Gal. iii. 13).

(6) Christ bearing our *sin :*

" Who His own self bare our sins in His body upon the tree " (1 Pet. ii. 24).

" Him who knew no sin He made to be sin on our behalf " (2 Cor. v. 21).

7. *Some suggested theories of the Atonement.* Several attempts have been made to frame a theory of the Atonement in which its saving power may be accounted for without supposing that Christ actually bore the guilt and penalty of sin in man's stead. Amongst these we may note the following:

(1) The theory that Christ saves men, not by bearing their guilt, but by a *perfect obedience,* which is set over against the disobedience of men (cf. Rom. v. 19). On this view the chief interest of the Cross is that it was the supreme and final instance of Christ's earthly obedience.

(2) The theory that Christ expressed in His Death a *perfect repentance* on behalf of men, so that it becomes possible for God to forgive sin. But, surely, to repent is an absolutely personal act: one may grieve for the sins of another, but that sorrow is not repentance.

(3) The theory that in the Cross we have the supreme *exhibition of the sinfulness of sin,* so that it saves by leading men to hate sin.

(4) The theory that in the Cross we see the crowning *exhibition of God's love for men,* in consequence of which they are won from sin to His service.

(5) The theory that the Death of Christ made His human experience complete, so that He has a *full and perfect sympathy* with men, and can act as the ideal Intercessor on their behalf.

Obviously each of these views is true as far as it goes, and it is a gain to have these elements of the truth emphasized ; but none of them does justice to more than one or two of the Scripture statements quoted above, for they all deny that Christ died in our stead.

8. *Some Objections urged against the Doctrine.* Before leaving the subject of the Atonement we ought to consider the two leading objections that are sometimes urged against it.

(1) Many have the feeling that *it is not just that one should bear the consequences of the sins of others.* But (*a*) The principle of sacrifice runs through life, and the world is full of vicarious suffering, i.e., the suffering of one as a substitute for others. If each individual were absolutely independent of others, justice might claim that each should bear his own burden. But, in actual fact, the world is so constituted that every life touches many others, and the sin of one brings pain and shame to others. Sometimes such undeserved suffering makes us think hardly of the world and its Ruler. At other times, as in the voluntary suffering of a mother on behalf of her children, it seems one of the divinest things in life. Now the sacrifice of Christ was perfectly voluntary (see John x. 18). If we do not feel that it is unjust that a mother should be allowed to suffer for her children, it is not unjust that Jesus Christ should be allowed to suffer for men. (*b*) It must also be remembered that the Son and the Father are one: we are not to think of God as making a victim of the Son,

for the Father, too, shared in the great sacrifice (see John iii. 16). It is one of the most suggestive facts about the Atonement that, if the world seems full of suffering and sorrow, the suffering, sorrow and sin touch its Maker too.

(2) It is also said that the doctrine of the Atonement is morally dangerous, seeing that *it may encourage men to think that they can sin with impunity*. It is sadly true that men of the baser sort have sometimes done so. Indeed, whole sects have sometimes fallen into *Antinomianism;* that is, they have thrown off morality itself, and have said in effect, " Let us sin that grace may abound " (cf. Rom. vi. 1), arguing that, if it is God's glory to forgive sin, the more scope we give Him to exercise this grace the greater will be His glory. But, obviously, this is a complete misunderstanding of the Atonement. God does not forgive men in their sins, but when they have parted from their sins by repentance. Faith in the Atonement is not merely to believe the fact that Christ died for sin, but to enter into the spirit of His Death and acknowledge that it is just that sin should be punished.

The outcome of a true faith in the Atonement will thus be just the reverse of Antinomianism. Christ's Death was a death to sin, and we share in that by faith. But, apart from that, at the Cross we see, as nowhere else, the sinfulness of sin and learn to hate it: and we also see, as nowhere else, the love of God ; so that gratitude and love will reinforce every motive of decency and shame to encourage us to live, no longer unto ourselves, but unto Him who for our sakes both died and rose again (see 2 Cor. v. 15).

E.—THE RESURRECTION

We have already seen that there is abundant evidence that the Resurrection was an actual historical fact. There are three ways in which it has an important bearing upon the salvation of man.

1. It immensely *strengthens our belief in the future life:* Death cannot end all, for at least one, who was

actually dead and buried, has come back from beyond the grave. By His Resurrection Christ has " brought life and incorruption to light " (2 Tim. i. 10). But such a belief affects a man's whole way of thinking, and makes it impossible for him to settle down to a merely animal or worldly life.

2. Because of the Resurrection we can both believe in and proclaim *a Living Christ* (see Rom. vi. 9). For us He is not merely one who lived, taught, and died centuries ago—He belongs to the present: He lives, loves, and works to-day. It has been well said that the crucifix is quite inadequate as the symbol of Christianity, for our Christ is no longer upon the Cross: He is not dead but risen. St. Paul can scarcely be charged with under-estimating the significance of Christ's Death, yet he will not allow his thought to stop short there: " It is Christ Jesus that died, yea rather, that was raised from the dead " (Rom. viii. 34). We owe more than can ever be told to the Death of Christ, but chiefly because it was followed by the Resurrection ; for it is the Resurrection that proves the greatness of the One who died, and it is His risen Life that enables Him to apply to men the merits of His Death, and to be their personal Friend and Helper. Cf. " For if, while we were enemies, we were reconciled to God through the death of His Son, much more, being reconciled, shall we be saved by His life " (Rom. v. 10).

3. The fact that Christ conquered Death is proof that *He also conquered Sin,* of which Death is the outcome and representative. Hence we can believe that on the Cross Sin sustained a mortal defeat. It still carries on a guerrilla war, and claims its victims in many directions, but the final issue is certain. Thus, the individual may reckon himself dead unto sin, but alive unto God (see Rom. vi. 11) ; and we may face the larger enterprises of the Church with the certainty of ultimate victory.

F.—THE ASCENSION

The triumphant Ascension and Exaltation of our Lord also inspire beliefs and hopes that make for our salvation.

1. Christ has now become *King* and has received again the glory that He had with the Father before the world was. He is no longer cramped and restricted by the limitations of His earthly life: all authority is His in heaven and on earth (see Matt. xxviii. 18) ; and, whatever may be the needs either of His people or of His Kingdom, He is able to meet them.

2. At the same time He is still our Saviour, Brother, Friend. He still is, and will for ever be, the God-man:

> He has raised our *human* nature
> In the clouds to God's right hand.

The work of His glorified life is still that of Salvation, for " He ever liveth to make intercession for (us) " (Heb. vii. 25). Hence He is called our *High Priest*. The Epistle to the Hebrews works out the analogy in detail: His earthly life made Him truly sympathetic and the fit Representative of men ; His sinlessness qualified Him to be both the spotless Sacrifice and the holy Priest ; the Sacrifice was offered on Calvary ; the Ascension was His entrance as High Priest into " the holiest of all " ; and His eternity makes both His sacrifice and His High-Priesthood eternal and unchangeable, so that earthly sacrifices and earthly priests are now unnecessary. We may therefore think of Him as a High Priest of infinite sympathy, standing before God for us. Inasmuch as our prayers are often foolish or defective, He intercedes on our behalf ; and, as our Representative, He bears before God the prayers which are offered in His name.

3. The Ascended Christ is still so far one with men that we find Him described, not simply as our Substitute or Representative, but as our *Forerunner,* who has gone in advance where we by His grace are eventually to follow Him (Heb. vi. 20). So, too, in the phrase, " Christ the *first-fruits* " (1 Cor. xv. 23), St. Paul describes Him as the beginning and the promise of a great harvest of glorified humanity. From this point of view Christ's present work is " to prepare a place " for us (John xiv. 2); and the final stage of His work will be to " come again " (John xiv. 3), and, in the Resurrection, " fashion anew

the body of our humiliation, that it may be conformed to the body of His glory " (Phil. iii. 21). Then, like a warrior who has subjugated some territory that he may hand it over as a new possession to his sovereign, Christ, having prepared a redeemed and glorified humanity, " shall deliver up the Kingdom to God, even the Father " (1 Cor. xv. 24), " that God may be all in all " (1 Cor. xv. 28).

CHAPTER VI

THE HOLY SPIRIT

HAVING studied at some length the Christian belief concerning God and Jesus Christ, we have now to consider the subject of the Holy Spirit, the Third Person in the Blessed Trinity.

Mention is made of the Spirit of God as early as the second verse of the Bible, and, as will be seen below, there are many other references to Him in the Old Testament ; but much the most important parts of our knowledge concerning Him are gathered from the words of our Lord at the Last Supper (see John xiv.-xvi.), and the experience of the disciples at Pentecost and in the years that followed.

A.—HIS NAME AND NATURE

1. *His Name.* The name of " Holy Spirit," or " Holy Ghost," is given to Him, not because the Father and the Son are less spiritual in their essence than He, but because we have no other way in which we can speak of Him save as a Spirit. We know that " God is a Spirit," yet the fact that He is both Sovereign and Father leads us, almost against our wills, to picture Him in thought, and to localize Him on the throne of the Universe: His spirituality is not our dominant thought concerning God the Father. Similarly, it is almost impossible to think of the Incarnate Son without picturing a human form. But in the case of the Holy Spirit there is no temptation to do

this, for no human analogy is ever used to describe His relationship to men. Hence we think of Him simply as a *Spirit*—immaterial, invisible, omnipresent.

2. *His Personality*. This pure spirituality is so marked that there is even a danger that we may lose sight of the fact that He is a *Person*, and conceive of Him as merely an *influence* emanating from God. The matter is of great importance, for if the Holy Spirit were not a Person it would be impossible to maintain the doctrine of the Trinity, and in that case it would be very difficult, if not impossible, to maintain the Divinity of our Lord, since a Trinity in the Godhead is much more intelligible philosophically than a Duality, or Godhead of two Persons. Unitarians, of course, deny the real Personality of the Spirit, and regard the personal references as mere personifications in speech, just as we personify Art when we speak of it as a mistress, or Fortune when we speak of it as a goddess.

The evidences of His Personality are as follows:

(1) He is linked with the Father and the Son in the Baptismal formula (Matt. xxviii. 19), and in the Benediction (2 Cor. xiii. 14).

(2) In the latter He is associated with a kind of blessing, namely, "fellowship" or "communion," which has no meaning except in the case of a person, for there cannot be fellowship with an influence.

(3) Personal actions are continually ascribed to Him, e.g., "The Spirit *said* unto Philip" (Acts viii. 29), and "Having been *forbidden* of the Holy Ghost to speak the word in Asia" (Acts xvi. 6).

3. *His Divinity*. There can be little question that the New Testament writers regard Him as *Divine*, the mere linking of His name with that of the Father and the Son being sufficient evidence of that. A statement of the most definite kind is also found in Acts v., where the lie to the Holy Ghost of verse 3 is spoken of as lie unto God in verse 4.

4. *His Subordination*. At the same time the New

Testament recognizes a certain order of rank among the Persons of the Trinity, the Spirit being *subordinate* to the Father and the Son. He is said to " proceed from " the Father (John xv. 26), and to be " sent " by the Father at the petition of the Son (John xiv. 16). He is also described in John xvi. 7, as sent by the Son.

B.—THE WORK OF THE HOLY SPIRIT

1. *The Teaching of the Old Testament.* (*a*) The Spirit is represented as God's Agent in *Creation* (see Gen. 1. 2, and Job xxxiii. 4). In view of this fact, it is very suggestive that He is described as operating in the Virgin Birth (Matt. i. 18, and Luke i. 35). The description of Him in the latter passage as " the Power of the Most High," or active Energy of God, should be noted.

(*b*) He is described as *inspiring* the special gifts of *national leaders,* such as the Judges (see Gen. xli. 38 ; Num. xi. 17, xxvii. 18 ; Judges, iii. 10, vi. 34, xi. 29 ; and 1 Sam. xvi. 13). This aspect of His work is specially prominent in the teaching of the Book of Isaiah concerning *the Messiah* and His equipment (see Isa. xi. 2 and lxi. 1). In the same way He is recognized as the source of the *inspiration of the Prophets* (see 1 Sam. x. 10 ; 1 Kings xxii. 24 ; Ezek, iii. 12, xi. 5, xxxvii. 1 ; and Micah iii. 8). Hence the statement concerning the Old Testament in 2 Peter i. 21, " Men spake from God, being moved by the Holy Ghost." Cf. also 1 Peter i. 11 and the words of the Creed, " who spake by the Prophets."

(*c*) The Spirit is also described as continually ministering to promote *holiness and spiritual life :* He strives with men (Gen. vi. 3) ; He equips them for sacred tasks (Ex. xxviii. 3 and xxxv. 31) ; He is the moral Instructor of the nation (Neh. ix. 20, 30) ; He is the source of inward and spiritual life (Ezek. xxxvi. 26, 27 and xxxvii. 14) ; and there is a remarkable prediction of a greater manifestation of His presence and power (Joel ii. 28, 29).

2. *The Teaching of John the Baptist*

The Baptist uttered one great saying concerning the

Spirit in his promise that Jesus should " baptize with the Holy Ghost and with *fire* " (Matt. iii. 11). The Spirit is here conceived of as the *Spirit of Fire* purifying and refining by burning up the dross of character.

3. *The Teaching of Jesus*

This is mainly found in His discourses at the Last Supper as recorded in John xiv-xvi.

(1) *The Comforter*. The name of " Comforter," beautiful as it is, is unfortunately very misleading as a translation of the word used by Jesus ; for the real meaning is one who is called to a man's side to support him and plead for him, much as a barrister does in court. The words *Advocate* and *Helper* suggested in the R.V. margin are much more suitable, though many prefer simply to reproduce the Greek word, and speak of the *Paraclete*.

It should be carefully noted that Jesus speaks of the Holy Spirit as " *another* Comforter " (John xiv. 16), implying that He is *another of the same kind* as Jesus Himself. That is, the Spirit was to be Christ's substitute, and to be to the disciples all that He had been as their Friend and Helper. But He was also to be more, for the departure of Jesus that the Spirit might come, was to be a gain to them (John xvi. 7). More particularly the gain was to consist in a more intimate companionship with the Spirit than had been possible with the human Jesus. They had companied with Jesus, and known Him from the outside ; but the Spirit was to dwell within them (see John xiv. 17). Perhaps the simplest way of conceiving of the Spirit of Christ is to think of Him as *Christ without any earthly body,* or as being all that Jesus was in tenderness, love, and helpfulness, without the limitations that restricted the earthly ministry of Jesus to a particular land and time ; for, as a Spirit, He can carry on the divine work in the hearts of men everywhere and through all the ages.

(2) *The Spirit of Truth*. " When He, the *Spirit of Truth,* is come, He shall guide you into all the truth " (John xvi. 13). The Apostolic Church must have sorely needed His teaching, for they had to wrestle with the great

problems suggested by Christ's Person and Death, and they had to carry forward and expand the teaching Jesus had given. On the strength of this promise the Church in all ages has claimed the help of the Spirit to guide it in its doctrine and its enterprises.

(3) *The Remembrancer*. He shall "bring to your *remembrance* all that I said unto you" (John xiv. 26). The divine aid needed by the writers of the Gospels would be mainly for the accurate reproduction of the teaching of Jesus, and their inspiration consisted mainly of the Spirit's work as Christ's Remembrancer.

(4) *The Spirit of Conviction*. "He will convict the world in respect of sin, and of righteousness, and of judgment" (John xvi. 8). That is, the Spirit was to compel men to acknowledge the reality of sin and of judgment, and admit the claims of righteousness ; so that, whatever power the preached Word may have to touch the hearts and consciences of men, it owes to Him.

(5) *The Spirit of Power*. "Ye shall receive *power*, when the Holy Ghost is come upon you" (Acts i. 8). This power was shown in the fact that these humble and, for the most part, ignorant men were able, through the Spirit, to touch the hearts and change the lives of multitudes of men and women, and almost to "turn the world upside down." The moral miracle of Conversion is so extraordinary as to justify the strange saying of Jesus that the works of the disciples should be even greater than His own (John xiv. 12).

4. *The Teaching of the Epistles*. Our Saviour traces to the Spirit both the conviction of sin (John xvi. 8) and the New Birth (John iii. 5). Similarly, in the Epistles the work of the Spirit is recognized in every stage of the personal Christian life: they describe *the Spirit in the hearts of men*.

(1) He creates the *faith* by which men recognize and confess the claims of Christ as the Divine Lord (1 Cor. xii. 3).

(2) It is the *witness* of the Spirit which gives a man the comforting assurance that He is a child of God (Rom. viii. 16).

(3) His presence in the heart is the " *seal* " by which God marks men as His own (Eph. i. 13).

(4) All *sanctification* of life is His work (Rom. xv. 16 and 2 Thess. ii. 13).

(5) Dwelling in the heart, He gives the right *direction* to life and prompts men to follow it (Rom. viii. 4 ; Gal. v. 16).

(6) He keeps the believer in his weakness, *interceding* on his behalf for the blessings most appropriate to his needs (Rom. viii. 27).

(7) The outcome of His life in the heart is seen in many choice graces of character, " the *fruit* of the Spirit " (Gal. v. 22).

(8) The experience of His presence in the heart here on earth is the " *earnest* " or " *pledge* " or first instalment of the perfected spiritual life for which we look in Heaven (2 Cor. i. 22).

The Epistles also throw light on *the relation of the Spirit to the Church*.

(1) The distinguishing purpose of the Christian Church, without which it cannot justify its existence, is to serve as the *Temple of the Holy Ghost* (1 Cor. iii. 16).

(2) He is the source of all *revelation* of the knowledge of God in the New Testament Church as in the Old (1 Cor. ii. 10 ; 1 Tim. iv. 1).

(3) He bestows upon individual members of the Church striking and varied *gifts* for the service of the whole (1 Cor. xii. 4-11).

(4) He continually *directs* the Church and its workers in their enterprises (Acts viii. 29, xiii. 2, xvi. 6, 7).

5. *The Spirit in the experience of the Early Church*. The work of the Spirit may also be studied in the experience of the Early Church as set forth in the New Testament, especially in the Book of the Acts. The promises of Christ and the teaching of the Epistles as to what the Spirit may be expected to do were abundantly confirmed in the first generation of Christianity.

(1) *Pentecost*. The disciples found the promises of their Lord more than fulfilled in the remarkable events of Pentecost. The Spirit did actually become to them a satisfying substitute for their Master, and proved Himself to be the Spirit of truth and of remembrance, the Spirit of conviction and of power. The following details should be noted: (*a*) The visible sign of the Spirit's presence was *a tongue of fire*—the symbol of burning utterance in the proclamation of the Gospel. (*b*) It sat upon *each* of them, men and women alike—a sign that the Spirit is not the monopoly of an ordained ministry. (*c*) It enabled them to speak in *many tongues*—a token of His world-wide mission.

(2) *Other Outpourings*. From time to time the experience of Pentecost was repeated, though in a less striking way in various groups of converts in many different localities (see Acts iv. 31, viii. 14-17, ix. 17, x. 44, xix. 1-7). Indeed, conversion to Christianity was hardly regarded as complete without it. The Spirit also continued to manifest His presence and power by the gift of miraculous *healing* (see Acts iii. 1-10, ix. 32-35, xiv. 8-10, xxviii. 8, 9).

(3) *Corinth*. From 1 Cor. xii. and xiv. it appears that the Church at Corinth was specially rich in many different spiritual gifts, some of higher and more enduring value to the Church than others.

6. *The Spirit in the Modern Church*. (1) *Lost Gifts*. The gift of *healing* appears to have lingered in isolated cases for two or three generations ; and there are some who believe that, if the Church were more worthy of its privileges, it might still exercise this gift. Is seems more likely, however, that the Spirit will suit His gifts to the

needs of each age ; and, in view of modern progress in medicine and surgery, the gift of healing is no longer an urgent need of the Church. If the Pentecostal gift of *tongues* is to be regarded as an equipment for missionary service, it is no longer of great importance now that the Gospel is printed and circulated in almost every known language. But, inasmuch as the Apostles do not appear to have continued to know and use these foreign tongues, the miracle seems to have been rather a prophecy of the universal proclamation of the Truth, than an equipment for it. Under stress of great spiritual excitement, something not unlike the Corinthian gift of ecstatic speech in a strange, and apparently unintelligible, language has been known in comparatively recent days.

(2) *Abiding Gifts.* If some of the Spirit's gifts were only temporary, there are other great gifts of His which the Church still needs, and will always need ; and in regard to these the experience of to-day corresponds with that of Apostolic times. Conversion is still an inward mystery, the work of the Spirit alone ; many claim to have experienced a " baptism of the Spirit " which has brought to them a new sense of spiritual joy and power ; those who are most successful in the winning of others agree in saying, " Yet not I, but the grace of God which was with me " ; and, lastly, in its movements of thought and in its great enterprises the Church still feels compelled to seek the wisdom and guidance of the Spirit, and does not seek them in vain.

CHAPTER VII

THE NATURE OF MAN

IF our Creed is to stand the test of practical life, it is quite as important to form a right conception of Man and his possibilities as to think truly and worthily concerning God. To some extent our conception of God will influence our belief concerning Man, and vice versa.

D

Perhaps the simplest way of studying the nature of Man is to examine his relationship to the Universe of which he forms a part, and to compare him and contrast him with the Creator and with various forms of created existence which we know, such as Animal Life and Matter.

A.—MAN'S RELATION TO THE CREATED WORLD

Man as a Creature. We saw in our study of Creation that, relatively to the Universe in which he lives, Man is a small and feeble creature. He is so far from being self-created that he comes into the world by no will of his own ; and so far from being self-sufficient that, from the first breath that he draws to the last, he is dependent on persons and things outside himself for the maintenance of his existence.

We saw, further, that in all probability there lie behind Man untold centuries of *gradual evolution*. In spite of his littleness Man can thus pride himself that he is " fearfully and wonderfully made," and that, up to the present, no higher order of life has appeared, at any rate upon the earth ; he is so far great that this beautiful world would seem to have been prepared expressly for his habitation.

We cannot say that there may not be creatures of a higher order in other worlds, and still less have we any right to say that there are not spiritual beings intermediate between God and Man. But there is nothing to suggest that any creature higher than Man is ever likely to be evolved upon the earth. We seem to have reached the limit of physical development ; as a creature Man appears to be *final :* the evolution of the present is only intellectual, moral and spiritual, with the aim of producing a higher type of Man, not a creature superior to Man. Century by century the race has gradually moved upward, and presumably it will continue to do so.

> These things shall be ! a loftier race
>   Than e'er the world has known shall rise,
> With flame of freedom in their souls
>   And light of knowledge in their eyes.

B.—MAN'S RELATION TO MATTER

(1) *His Body.* On one side Man is part of the material world. As the Bible puts it, he is dust, taken out of the ground (Gen. iii. 19). Every atom of food by which his frame is built up has come from the earth, some through the instrumentality of living plants, e.g., wheat or fruit, and some through the instrumentality of other animals, e.g., flesh foods and milk. At death the body decays, and literally returns to the earth and becomes part of it once more.

(2) *His Soul.* Yet man is conscious that his body is not his real self. The material substances that compose the body and the brain can be analysed, weighed, and measured ; but thoughts, affections, desires and aspirations are not material ; and cannot be analysed by any process of the laboratory. Sound is a material thing, a wave of air. But its result when it has passed into the brain is neither a wave nor air, but a note of music. The caress in which a baby strokes its mother's face is a physical thing, and its force might be expressed as so many ounces of soft matter at a certain temperature moving across the face at a certain speed. But in the mother's heart it becomes transformed into something which cannot be expressed in any such terms, the glow of love. Our inner life consists of thoughts, feelings, and desires, none of which are material, hence we say that the real self or soul is something which is not material.

(3) *The Relation of Soul and Body.* Though the soul and the body are so different they are closely related and dependent upon each other. Without the soul the body is mere decaying matter, without the body the soul could not live its life in a material world. The body may be called the home or dwelling-place of the soul, but it is even more its instrument: it conveys to the soul all impressions from without, through it the soul executes its will, and through it the soul communicates with other souls. But the soul is the higher and predominant partner, it is the real self: we should not say that man *has* a soul— he *is* a soul and *has* a body.

A number of terms are employed to describe the different parts of Man's nature, and both in Scripture and in popular speech they are often used loosely and ambiguously: *heart, mind, soul* and *spirit* may all be used in much the same sense ; and the Bible also speaks of the *bowels* and the *reins,* or kidneys, as the seat of the feelings and affections. The meaning of these terms varies greatly with the context. For instance the word *soul* may mean simply a living man, as in " All the souls of the house of Jacob, which came into Egypt, were threescore and ten " (Gen. xlvi. 27). Sometimes the soul is the man's own self, e.g., " I will say to my soul, Soul, thou hast much goods laid up for many years " (Luke xii. 19). Or again, the soul may be the moral and spiritual part of the man, e.g., " Fleshly lusts, which war against the soul " (1 Peter ii. 11) and " The Shepherd and Bishop of your souls " (1 Peter ii. 25).

In considering the essential nature of Man we may reduce the terms to three, Body, Soul, and Spirit ; and probably to two, Body and Spirit, or Body and Soul. Man is generally represented as consisting of three elements ; but it has been aptly said that the most accurate illustration of his constitution is not a three-storied building, but a two-storied building with a skylight in the roof. On this view he consists of Body and Soul, the Soul being called the Mind in so far as it looks out upon the world, and the Spirit in so far as it looks up towards Heaven.

C.—MAN'S RELATION TO THE BRUTES

(1) *His Kinship.* On any theory of the origin of Man it is an obvious fact that in his physical constitution he very closely resembles other animals. There is not an organ, possibly not a bone, in his body which has not its counterpart in other animals. There are, it is true, some notable differences even on the physical side: Man walks erect, and his brain is heavier and more elaborate in its structure than that of the animals that most nearly approach him. Yet substantially Man's physical constitution, his physical appetites and desires, and the natural processes of his birth, life, and death, are the

same as those of many other animals. The Theory of Evolution is merely an attempt to account for these resemblances, which were recognized long before the theory was suggested.

(2) *Marked Differences*. In spite of this kinship, there is an almost immeasurable gap between Man and the brutes. The comparison must, of course, be made between Man at his best and the brutes at their best. Some degraded savages seem hardly distinguishable from the wild beasts of their forests: but even in them there is a capacity for civilization, education, and refinement that does not exist in the brutes. (*a*) *Intelligence* is far more highly developed in Man. Dogs and horses are sometimes highly intelligent, yet their education cannot be carried beyond the learning of a simple routine or the performance of a few tricks. Ants and bees show a very remarkable practical skill and a highly developed social organization. Yet Man alone makes tools and weapons, fashions clothes, kindles fire, cooks his food, and makes use of such great natural forces as steam and electricity. (*b*) *Language* of a kind appears to exist amongst animals, but it is only with Man that it has been developed to become a medium for complex thought and intellectual or witty conversation. (*c*) *Consciousness* exists among the animals, that is, they are aware of feelings of pleasure or pain, and can respond to impressions from without. But there is no evidence of *self-consciousness* in them, that is, no evidence that they are able to detach themselves from their surroundings and recognize themselves as something distinct from the rest of the Universe ; and no evidence that they are able to contemplate the Universe, or form any connected idea of it. (*d*) *Beauty* apparently makes no appeal to animals, except that some are said to be attracted by music. There is no evidence that the most intelligent dog or horse ever *sees* a landscape, still less that he recognizes in it a thing of beauty. (*e*) Some animals are capable of great devotion and *affection,* but their love and sympathy are of the simplest and crudest kind ; they have no capacity for the complex emotions of human life. (*f*) Some dogs possess the rudiments of a *moral sense,* and appear to feel guilt

and shame. But they have no capacity for a complex morality, such as is found in a human community with its many relationships, each of them involving some kind of duty to friends or neighbours or the State. (*g*) Man alone is capable of wonder, awe, and *worship*. He alone cherishes ideals and aspires, and he alone prays.

(3) *Man's lordship*. It is in keeping with this superiority that the Bible represents Man as the lord of Creation (Gen. ix. 1 - 3). The Evolutionary Theory equally admits his claim to the first place amongst the living creatures that inhabit the world. Man has clearly proved his lordship by impressing the more useful and tractable of the animals into his service, and by inventing weapons to which the most ferocious can offer no resistance.

D.—MAN'S RELATION TO GOD

(1) *His Dependence*. As a creature, and a little creature, Man is necessarily dependent upon God. He is, indeed, so insignificantly small that his attitude towards God should always include an element of humble awe: " God is in heaven, and thou upon earth: therefore let thy words be few " (Eccles. v. 2).

(2) *Made in God's Image*. In spite of the infinite differences we have the assurance of the Bible that there is a fundamental likeness between Man and God, and that Man was *made in the image of God* (see Gen. i. 27). It is sometimes sneeringly said that the truth is rather that Man has made God in *his* image, and conjured up for himself a Deity who is merely a magnified man. But the God of the Bible, though we are often compelled to speak of Him by means of imperfect human analogies, is far from being a magnified man.

That the presence of the image of God in Man is not inconceivable and not derogatory to God may be shown by comparing a candle flame with the sun. The sun is almost immeasurably distant and inconceivably vast, the candle flame is hardly an inch in length. The sun is an immense globe, the candle flame narrow and tapering. The sun appears to depend on no source of heat and light outside itself, the candle flame has to renew itself from moment to moment by drawing on the substance of the candle. Yet these two objects, so different, agree in two of the most remarkable properties: each gives out light and heat. Further, the candle may be said to be created by the sun, for it is the bottled-up sunshine of other days. It would not be amiss to say that the sun has created the candle flame in its own image.

Similarly, we find in Man three remarkable characteristics which, as we have already seen, are conspicuous in the Nature of God: (1) *Intelligence* or *Reason*, (2) *Love*, (3) *the capacity for Goodness*. To claim that in these three particulars God has made Man in His own image is not to deny that God infinitely transcends Man and differs from him in numberless ways. This image of God is often defaced or obscured, and it is sometimes latent and undeveloped, but these are not reasons for denying its existence.

(3) *God's Child*. The teaching of Jesus that God is our Father carries us still further. If Man is dependent upon God, it may be with the simple and confident dependence of a child upon a loving Father. If God has made Man, it is by imparting something of His own eternal Life and Being. But if Man has in him something of the likeness of God, it is because he is God's child.

A son is still the son of his father even though he does not know it, and even though he repudiates the relationship ; and so far all men are sons of God. But there is also a conscious sonship into which men may enter by faith, the sonship of believers (see John i. 12).

E.—MAN'S RELATION TO THE RACE

(1) *Individual Personality*. Each man is conscious that he exists as a separate and distinct individual, so that he can say of himself, " *I* am *I,* a being different from every other being in existence." No two individuals are really alike, and when the children of a family most closely resemble one another each has his own will, tastes, disposition and characteristics. Even in a rare case like that

of the Siamese Twins, in which two persons are physically inseparable, there are still two lives and not one, with two distinct personalities, two wills, and two characters.

This fact that we feel ourselves to be separate individuals is of great importance when we come to consider the question of the freedom of Man's will and his moral responsibility.

(2) *Human Relationships.* But, in spite of our sense of individuality, no one of us is really isolated from his fellows. We are born into a world of men and women, to some of whom we are related by blood, and to others of whom we are bound by ties of friendship and in other ways. No man can ever live an entirely independent life. The most selfish and exclusive and most solitary are touched on some side of their being by other lives. The man who hates his kind and shuts himself away from them cannot live as if others did not exist, for his hatred of them is part of his life. In the days of his greatest solitude Robinson Crusoe's life was still touched by his fellows, for the memory of his friends and the longing to rejoin them were always with him. Our lives are never self-contained: we throw out filaments that strike root in other lives, and, especially in the case of those whom we love, part of our life is lived in them.

This fact that Man is a *social being* will be found to be one of the great reasons for the existence of the Christian Church; for, like the natural human life, the spiritual life of men cannot be lived in isolation.

(3) *The Solidarity of the Race.* We seem to be bound together in a still deeper sense; for there are many things that suggest that beneath the surface all humanity is really one. Each island in an archipelago appears to be separate and distinct, with its own peculiar characteristics. Yet a few hundred feet below the surface all the islands meet in the one sea-bottom, and their unity is so real that an earthquake which shakes one will make itself felt in all the rest. The separate leaves of a tree have a real individuality; yet they all belong to the same tree, and the same life flows through them all. Modern thought

attaches increasing importance to what is called _the Solidarity of the Race,_ or the fact that the Race is not merely a collection of individuals but a living whole. Mankind does not correspond to a number of balls in a basket, touching one another at various points, but otherwise independent of each other ; it more nearly resembles a living organism in which the various parts have a living connexion with each other, like the cells of the body or the leaves of a tree.

This fact has important consequences in three ways:

(*a*) It helps to account for the unmerited suffering which comes to some through the wrongdoing of others.

(*b*) It will be found to throw light on the great questions of Universal Sin and Guilt and Universal Redemption.

(*c*) It makes it clear that God's purpose of Salvation includes the regeneration of the community as well as the conversion of individuals.

F.—MAN'S RELATION TO THE PAST

(1) *Heredity.* Every man at birth inherits a great legacy from the past. He is "heir to all the ages," first, in the obvious sense that he is free to profit by the inventions, the art and the literature of the past (cf. John iv. 38); and also in the sense that he himself is to some extent an embodiment and reproduction of all the bygone generations. It is said that there can be traced in the development of an infant most of the stages by which Man has moved upward. Ardent advocates of the theory of Evolution delight to point out resemblances between Man and his animal ancestors, not only in details of his bodily structure, such as the rudimentary tail, but also in many tricks of movement, such as the clinging instinct of a baby, and in the ungoverned tempers and the tendency to cruelty so often found in children.

More particularly we can trace resemblances to our immediate ancestors for three or four generations back. The process of Heredity is somewhat irregular, so that a particular trait may reproduce itself in some members of a family and not in the rest, or it may lie hidden for a generation or two and then appear again.

(2) *The range of Heredity.* The principle of Heredity applies to every part of our nature. The physical resemblances between parents and their children are often very marked. The transmission of intellectual gifts is not so certain, for, though in a few cases brilliant parents have produced brilliant offspring, it is not always the case ; and, on the other hand, a number of the intellectual geniuses have appeared quite suddenly and unaccountably. Heredity certainly applies to character and disposition, though not with much precision. The child of devout parents is not always markedly religious, but the religious temperament of his parents may re-appear in the form of a passion for music or for poetry. St. Paul teaches in 1 Cor. vii. 14 that the children of a Christian father or mother are, in some sense, holy.

(3) *Is Heredity just ?* Children suffer for the sins of their fathers, and the child of a libertine may start in life tainted in blood, and feeble mentally and morally as well as physically. Is it just?

It should be remembered that:

(*a*) There is a Heredity of *good* as well as of evil, and in the immense majority of cases the heritage of good far exceeds the heritage of evil.

(*b*) What Heredity produces is a *tendency,* and in most cases only a tendency. Special precautions may be needed to prevent a physical tendency from developing into actual disease, and special grace is needed to prevent the moral tendency from developing into actual sin ; but it is not impossible to hold either tendency in check.

(*c*) No man is the slave of Heredity. He is the child of his parents, but he is more—he is *himself,* in part a new creation, with a will of his own and the opportunity to exercise it.

The Law of Heredity will be found to be of special importance when we come to consider the question of Original Sin.

G.—MAN'S RELATION TO CIRCUMSTANCES OR TO " FATE "

No question concerning Man, not even the question of Immortality, is of greater importance than that of *Free Will.* Is he a free agent, responsible for his actions, or is he the slave of circumstances and of " Fate " ?

The problem has exercised the minds of men from the beginning ; and unbelief to-day often dismisses the whole question of religion and of moral responsibility by the simple assertion that Man is not really free.

(1) The *first objection commonly urged is that, if Man is free, to that extent God ceases to be Sovereign in the Universe ;* it is impossible for God to be Absolute Ruler if Man is at liberty to do as he chooses.

But it may be replied that God may choose to forgo His Sovereignty within certain small limits, just as many parents are willing to surrender one room in the house for the free use of their children. The Christian contends that God has done so, and done so with a great purpose. Nature glorifies God as a vast system that obeys Him absolutely. But the obedience of Nature is mechanical, it cannot be otherwise. In giving freedom to Man God is seeking to raise up beings who will glorify Him by an obedience that is perfectly free and voluntary, the obedience of choice.

(2) The *second objection* is that *throughout the Universe we find the Law of Cause and Effect working exactly :* we can trace and measure a cause for every effect that we see, and an effect following every cause. We know that even the weather, capricious as it seems to be, is the result of certain quite definite but complicated causes ; and if we only knew all the causes we should be able to forecast the weather with absolute accuracy. It is claimed that the life of Man is no exception to this rule, and that his deeds are the results of various influences acting upon him at a given moment, and not the result of his own free will. A healthy child is the result of healthy parentage plus wholesome diet and surroundings. Similarly, it is said, a criminal is simply the result of vicious parentage, bad training, and bad surroundings.

There is much weight in this objection, and *it cannot be denied that in many ways a man's life is determined for him and is beyond his own control*. This is perfectly clear, first, in regard to the *general course of his career*. He does not choose his parents, or the time or place of his birth, or the time of his death. His upbringing and education are in the hands of others. His environment may be one of great opportunity or one of great difficulty. At every turn his life is affected by circumstances over which he has no control. Shortness of stature, a delicate constitution, the lack of money, or the lack of influence may shut him out from certain careers. All along the line he is met by the unexpected and, apparently, accidental events, so that few men's lives at all correspond to the dreams and plans of their early days. The death of some relative, the whim of an employer, the " lottery " of marriage, a fall in the street—all these and a thousand other things may completely change his career. Some meet with extraordinary " luck " in every enterprise ; others, equally capable and hard-working, are dogged by misfortune all their days.

As regards the general course of life our freedom is thus very limited, and may be compared to the freedom of our movements on board a railway train: we may do much as we choose within the limits of the carriage, but all the time we are being carried forward by a power far greater than ourselves. In their larger aspects our lives are in the hands of God, and " He putteth down one, and lifteth up another " (Psa. lxxv. 7).

It is equally clear that *even in the moral sphere a man's life is largely shaped by influences other than a carefully reasoned choice*. Even whilst he knows that he is free to choose one course, he feels certain influences urging him to another. Of two possible lines of conduct open to him one is a line of less resistance than the other, and, generally speaking, that is the line that he will take. Usually a man does wrong because it seems to him easier and more pleasant than to do right. The influences that make some line the line of least resistance are generally two. (*a*) Public opinion, or the influence of a man's

" set," is a powerful driving force. (*b*) His past actions have created in him a certain kind of inclination, or habit, which it requires no effort to indulge. In the choice that men make, good or evil, they are chiefly decided by these two considerations.

It may be asked in this case, *What freedom remains ?* Man's Freedom consists in this, that, whilst he often allows these influences to guide him, he is *not* at their mercy and he *knows* that he is not—it is easy to yield to them, but it is not impossible to resist them.

The evidence that in this sense Man is morally free consists of the facts of experience, namely, that:

(*a*) Every man knows and feels in his own mind that he is at liberty to choose as he wills.

(*b*) All human society, all law and government, assume that a man can control his personal actions, and hold him responsible for doing so. Only infants and the insane are regarded as " not responsible."

(*c*) Thousands of instances prove that a man can, if he will, break with his past and defy the opinion of his friends. He can be successfully appealed to to change his course of life, and in this power to deliberately adopt a new ideal of life there is a fundamental difference between the most bestial of men and a pig, or between the most savage of men and a wolf or a shark.

Inseparable from Moral Freedom is *Moral Responsibility*. It is on this fact that the whole doctrine of Sin rests. At this point it need only be said that a man's responsibility corresponds exactly to his freedom: he is not morally guilty for deeds, however evil, which he does under irresistible compulsion.

H.—MAN'S RELATION TO THE FUTURE—IMMORTALITY

At this point we can only take up the general question, " If a man die, shall he live again?" and state the reasons for believing that death does not end all. The very important questions as to the endless duration and the character of the life beyond must be left for discussion in Chapter XII.

1. *The Teaching of the Bible*

The Bible nowhere attempts to prove the continuance of life after death. It assumes it, just as it assumes the existence of God. In the Old Testament the conception of the future is very dim: *Sheol,* or the Grave, or the Underworld, is a region of gloomy and shadowy existence which hardly deserves the name of life, for it is scarcely more than non-extinction (see Psa. vi. 5 and Isa. xxxviii. 18).

Yet the Old Testament doctrine that Man is made in the *image of God* gives us a very important reason for believing in the future life: for if his life is derived from God it is hardly conceivable that it can end with death.

In the interval between the two Testaments the belief concerning the future became much more definite. In our Saviour's day there was a very clear belief in a bodily *resurrection,* though the Sadducees rejected it. But throughout the New Testament it is assumed that life continues after death, and that its great issues are determined then.

The New Testament affords us important direct evidence that death does not end all in the facts of:

(*a*) The *Resurrection* of Jesus from the dead.

(*b*) The three instances in which Jesus *raised the dead* to life, all of which become credible in the light of the Resurrection of Jesus Himself.

2. *General Reasoning*

(*a*) The hope of the future is *an almost universal instinct.* In some instances, e.g., in Confucianism, belief in the spirits of the departed is even more definite than belief in God. Amongst many primitive races the belief in the spirits of the dead and in ghosts is said to have given rise to such faith as they have in other unseen spirits and in gods. In India the common belief takes the form of a succession of lives, or re-incarnations in other animals, until at last the soul is re-absorbed and lost in the stream of Divine Being. Even the more philosophic Buddhism, which looks for an ultimate return to nothingness, teaches that, for a time at least, something survives.

To this it is sometimes replied that such an instinctive belief only indicates that we cannot imagine ourselves as ceasing to exist, that is, we cannot picture a blank nothingness, or imagine what our thoughts and feelings will be when we have ceased to be able to think and feel.

(b) A sounder reason for believing in the future life is that when we consider *the nature of conscious human life* it is impossible to see why it should end with the death of the body. It is said that a race of savages unfamiliar with the horse at first took the horse and its rider for one animal, and could not imagine their existence apart. Body and soul are no more inseparable than the horse and its rider, or the works of the watch and its case. In the present material world the soul admittedly requires a physical body to be its tenement and its instrument. But with the decay of the tenement the soul need not decay ; and, in actual fact, a man often remains very alert mentally and spiritually in spite of great age and physical decrepitude.

It may be said that this line of reasoning implies a future life for animals as well as for men. The Christian belief is that there is a fundamental spiritual difference between Man and other animals. Yet it is not inconceivable that there may be a future for them—many have held this belief, including John Wesley. It should be noted, however, that man is *self-conscious,* and animals are not. We know what it is to be in England by our bodies, but in Australia in our thoughts, that is, there is something in us which is independent of *Space*. Similarly, we can think at the same time of two periods centuries apart and compare them, that is, there is something in us that can stand outside *Time* and watch its course. This something which belongs to neither Space nor Time must surely be spiritual and immortal.

(c) Another most important consideration is that, *if death ends all, human life becomes meaningless*. Much of the suffering of life appears cruel and unjust, if there is no future in which the injustices of the present will be redressed. Human suffering becomes worthless as a discipline, and, for the most part, inconsistent with the goodness of God, if there is no future life in which the trained and disciplined powers are to be exercised. Human affections are a cruel mockery, if there is no continuance and renewal of them beyond the grave. To abandon the belief reduces life to meaningless confusion ; and, sooner or later, those who have done so have found that the Universe appears so vast and so cold, and both they and their fellows appear so insignificant and so transient, that all effort is paralysed—it is not worth while to try to make anything of such a life.

(*d*) Very few men, and probably none of any intellectual and moral worth, completely lose the *craving* for a future life, even though it may be reduced to the mere desire to survive in the lives of others, as it is expressed in George Eliot's lines:

> Oh, may I join the choir invisible
> Of those immortal dead who live again
> In minds made better by their presence.

(*e*) Ultimately we have to fall back on *faith in God*. Nothing but the actual experience of death can enable us to know with clear and certain knowledge what lies beyond. But it is inconceivable that all life can be meaningless and Man's greatest hope a baseless dream.

> Thou wilt not leave us in the dust :
> Thou madest man, he knows not why,
> He thinks he was not made to die ;
> And thou hast made him : thou art just.
>
> —*Tennyson.*

(*f*) Those, however, who have reached a glad experience of *present fellowship with God* through Christ have another argument which is conclusive, at any rate for them: " Christ in you " is " the hope of glory " (Col. i. 27) ; " Neither death nor life . . . shall be able to separate us from the love of God which is in Christ Jesus our Lord " (Rom. viii. 38, 39), for the mere death of the body cannot destroy that part of us which already lives with God and knows His personal love.

CHAPTER VIII

Sin

It is a wonderful conception of man and his destiny that we find in the Bible. Yet a very limited experience of life suffices to show that an evil principle has entered the Universe, which is the marring both of the world and of the race. This evil principle is known as Sin.

A.—DEFINITIONS AND DESCRIPTIONS OF SIN

It will help us to gain a clear conception of Sin if we compare together various definitions of it which are generally current.

(1) Some describe Sin as a mere *defect* or *lack*, not a positive thing at all, but simply the absence of goodness, just as darkness is the absence of light. This, however, is not true to experience, for there can be few who are not conscious of evil impulses that are distinctly positive and malignant. Hatred, for instance, is far more than the absence of love ; for the absence of love is only indifference to another, not a positive desire to injure him.

(2) Others describe Sin as the *trace of the brute* in man, the remnants of his savage animal ancestry. There are some fierce and cruel instincts of which this is an apt description. Yet there are many kinds of Sin which cannot be brought under this definition, e.g., untruth, disloyalty, treachery. And, even in the case of the sensual passions in which we seem to come nearest to the brutes, it is only in men that they become degrading vices : animals satisfy their appetites, but they do not become enslaved to them. The serious objection to such a definition is that it regards Sin as something inevitable, for which we are not responsible, and which will gradually correct itself as the race progresses.

(3) Others describe all Sin as *Selfishness*. Probably all forms of Sin are in some sense self-seeking. Yet the fiendish impulse which prompts a man to mock at virtue

and corrupt the innocent, e.g., by teaching a lad to drink and gamble, is not selfish, except in the modified sense that it is self against God and goodness.

(4) The Bible definition is given in the words " Sin is *lawlessness* " (1 John iii. 4), that is, the refusal to be controlled, or repudiation of the Law and Sovereignty of God. This covers all forms of Sin, e.g., hatred, lust, pride, unbelief, contempt of virtue, and the rest.

The essential point in this definition is that it regards all Sin as ultimately against *God*. This is not to say that we do not also sin against others. Our sins may be (*a*) against *ourselves*, e.g., degrading self-indulgence ; (*b*) against *others*, e.g., theft, deceit, cruelty ; (*c*) against God, e.g., blasphemy, unbelief, rebellion. Yet even the first and the second are also sins against God. For in degrading ourselves we both disappoint God in in His great purpose concerning us, and deface the image of God which is stamped upon us. Compare with this disappointment the mother's feeling of sorrow when her son becomes a drunkard or a criminal. As regards sins against others, in corrupting our fellow-creatures we defile their nature, which is meant to be a temple of God ; and, in injuring them, we wrong the God who loves them and whose children they are. Compare with this a father's feeling of pain and indignation when his child is ill-treated. Hence we can understand the striking words of Psa. li. 4: " Against Thee, Thee only, have I sinned, and done this evil in Thy sight." David had sinned grievously against both Uriah and Bath-sheba, and he had also sinned against himself ; but he felt that he had sinned even more against God, both by disappointing God's purpose concerning him, and also in injuring those whom God had made and for whom He cared.

No definition of Sin accords with the statements of Scripture, or accounts for men's sense of guilt, which does not regard Sin as essentially Sin against *God*. Many prefer to reserve the word exclusively for the Godward aspect of our offences, and speak of offences against men as wrongs or injuries or crimes rather than sins.

There are obviously many *forms of Sin*. We can dis-
dinguish between positive and negative sins, that is, sins
of commission and sins of omission ; and Sin may be not
only in deed, but in word, thought, desire, or motive.

B.—THE ORIGIN OF SIN

(1) Many have sought the origin of Sin in man's
material nature, and have regarded it as inherent in the
flesh and inseparable from the earthly *body*. This theory
appears to find some support in Scripture, for St. Paul
frequently describes the sinful life as life " after the flesh "
(Rom. viii. 4, 5). But St. Paul's use of the word *flesh*
is peculiar, and he means by it not the literal flesh and
blood, but the nature of Man as a whole apart from Divine
influence. That he does not regard the material body as
in itself sinful and the source of Sin is clear from the
following facts: (*a*) His list of the " works of the flesh "
(Gal. v. 19 - 21) includes idolatry, sorcery, enmities,
heresies, &c., which certainly do not belong to the body.
(*b*) He describes the body as sacred, the temple of the
Holy Ghost (1 Cor. vi. 19, 20). (*c*) The body, glorified
by the Resurrection, is to have a place in the life of
Heaven.

(2) As already mentioned the theory of Evolution describes Sin as *the heritage from man's animal ancestors*.
This may be true in part, but it fails to account for many
forms of Sin, and does not explain the sense of shame and
guilt.

(3) Coming to the *Bible doctrine of Sin* the venerable
story of the Fall (Gen. iii.) describes Sin as originating in
a voluntary choice of evil on the part of our first parents,
which created a tendency or bias towards evil that has
been transmitted to all their descendants. It makes no
difference to its teaching concerning Sin whether this story
is treated as literal history or as a quaint parable. Whatever the actual facts may have been, Sin presents itself
to every one in some such choice between obedience and
disobedience, and must have come to the first man in
a similar way.

The following points should be noted in this story of the *Fall :*

(*a*) Man was made *innocent,* that is, neither good nor evil in the full sense of the terms.

(*b*) He was submitted to a *moral test.* The forbidden tree may stand for any prohibited thing. It is called " the tree of knowledge of good and evil," not because its fruit was in any way unique, but because the fact that it was prohibited brought Adam and Eve face to face with the *choice* between obedience and disobedience, and so taught them the difference between good and evil. The first little prohibition which compels a child to make this choice is a " tree of the knowledge of good and evil " for him.

(*c*) They learnt the difference by *disobeying,* and so far there is truth in the statement that the Fall was a fall *upward,* for there was progress in it, seeing that they passed from the sphere of mere innocence into that of moral life. But the lesson might have been learnt equally well by *obedience,* and that would have started Man upon a happy instead of an unhappy moral progress.

(*d*) *God's purpose* in so testing them was a great and gracious one. Goodness is so far above innocence that it was worth while to face the risk of Sin in order to attain Virtue ; just as a loving parent exposes his child to certain risks to health and morals in the endeavour to make a man of him. If it had not been made possible for Man to sin he could never have been good, he would have remained only innocent and harmless.

(*e*) The essence of our parents' sin was *disobedience,* and needless disobedience, against a good and *loving* God.

(*f*) The *consequences* of their sin require fuller treatment in a separate section.

C.—THE CONSEQUENCES OF SIN

The Bible describes many painful and evil consequences as flowing from Sin, and they may be found in germ in the story of the Fall.

(1) *Guilt*. The statement that Adam and Eve knew that they were naked (Gen. iii. 7) represents the awakening of shame, the painful consciousness of guilt, the feeling that a man sometimes has of despising and hating himself when he realizes that he has sinned. The hiding in the garden and the aprons of fig-leaves represent the attempts that men make to hide their true selves from God, from their neighbours, and even from themselves, when once they have become conscious of Sin.

(2) *Separation from God*. Just as a child instinctively feels that wrongdoing raises a barrier between himself and his father, a barrier that is not mere fear of punishment, one of the immediate results of Sin is that the soul feels itself alienated from God. This is represented in the story by expulsion from Eden.

(3) *The curse*. The Bible speaks of a curse that came upon the ground as the result of the Fall (Gen. iii. 17 - 19). This is its explanation of the strange " contrariness " of things that men so frequently experience, as a result of which our labour often seems hard, repulsive and futile : our plans go wrong, circumstances arise that baffle us, the rewards of life are snatched from us just when we are on the point of winning them, and in many ways we find this a shortcoming and disappointing world. The teaching of Scripture is that the world is blighted by Sin (see Rom. viii. 19 - 22).

(4) *Pain and Death*. It is also the teaching of the Bible that many experiences of life, e.g., childbirth (see Gen. iii. 16), have a painful character that they need not have had ; and that death, even if it is not the direct result of Sin, has become a dark and dread ordeal because of Sin (see 1 Cor. xv. 56).

(5) *Widespread Consequences*. It is an evident fact of life that the consequences of Sin touch others besides the sinner. This is represented in the story of the Fall by the fact that the sin of Adam and Eve affected their offspring as well as themselves, for they all suffered by the exclusion from Eden and the separation from God.

(6) *Sinfulness of heart*. The worst of all the results of Sin is that the act of Sin taints or warps the nature and creates a *sinful disposition,* which shows itself in a sinful habit. "Virtue is its own reward," in the sense that a good deed tends to create a love of goodness and an inclination towards it ; and Sin is its own punishment, in the sense that it corrupts the nature and perverts the taste, so that with each new evil deed the inclination towards evil becomes more powerful. The transmission of these consequences of Sin to others must be treated in another section.

D.—THE TRANSMISSION OF SIN AND ORIGINAL SIN

Few doctrines of Christianity have been the subject of more bitter criticism than that of *Original Sin*. But there is none that finds surer warrant in the actual facts of life and experience. It is easy, however, to state the doctrine in terms that accord with neither truth nor justice.

(1) The term *Original Guilt,* which is seldom used now, is particularly liable to misunderstanding. If the word *guilt* is used in its proper sense it is impossible that a child can be guilty of the sin of his father. What is true is that the painful and shameful consequences of a father's sin descend to his child. The family of a convict necessarily suffer shame, and often suffer privation, because of his crime, though the world does not regard them as guilty. It often happened in olden days in the case of a dangerous criminal or agitator that both he and his descendants were banished from the state in perpetuity.

The meaning of Original Guilt is therefore that the pains and penalties of the first sin, and especially the alienation from God which resulted from it, have passed on to succeeding generations. If it be said that this is unjust, it may be replied that:

(*a*) It is in keeping with the actual facts of life.

(*b*) It is counterbalanced by a vast amount of unearned good which children receive from their forefathers.

(*c*) As regards alienation from God, the first sin is cancelled, for all who wish to be restored to fellowship with

God, by the obedience and the sacrifice of Christ (Rom. v. 19).

(2) Quite distinct from Original Guilt is *Original Sin*, or inborn sinfulness. The doctrine of Heredity makes us familiar with the fact that a man may transmit to his descendants his moral and spiritual as well as his physical characteristics. By Original Sin, or Birth Sin, we mean that every human being inherits from the past a sinful taint, a bias towards evil.

The justification for the doctrine is in the facts of actual life. In every department of life our first tendency is to do things wrongly; and even in such things as walking, writing and cricket we begin with wrong movements, and have slowly to learn the right ones. So, too, in the moral sphere it often appears easier and more natural for us to do wrong than to do right; generally speaking, it requires no effort to do wrong. This tendency to evil is so universal that a new community drafts laws and regulations with suitable pains and penalties as soon as it is constituted; and a man bequeathing property on trust inserts provisions against the abuse of it, even though the persons concerned are not yet born.

The extent of this evil taint or bias is described by the phrase *Total Depravity*. It is often misunderstood, and must not be taken to mean that man is born wholly evil, and is as bad as Sin and corruption can make him. Its proper meaning is that man's nature is tainted by Sin in every part of it—so that body, mind, and spirit have all some inclination to evil and any one of them may become a source of actual sin.

It cannot be too carefully noted that, like many other inherited traits, Original Sin is only a *tendency,* and need not become actual sin. It makes virtue more difficult for us, and necessitates watchfulness in guarding against it; but, though in probably every case, except that of Jesus Christ, it has become actual sin, there is no necessary reason why it should do so.

Our belief in Original Sin should also be balanced by

the belief in *Original Good*. If there is a heredity of evil, there is also a heredity of good. This takes two forms:

(*a*) Good parents transmit many good and sound moral qualities to their offspring.

(*b*) There is a second Head of the Race, Jesus Christ, " the last Adam," and from Him there enters into human nature a good strain (see Rom. v. 12 - 21). It is because of this that there is " a light which lighteth every man, coming into the world " (John i. 9).

So qualified, the doctrine of Original Sin requires little Bible support, for it is simply a statement of the actual, undeniable, facts of life. It is well illustrated by Browning's poem *Gold Hair :*

> The candid incline to surmise of late
>   That the Christian faith proves false, I find.
>
> I still to suppose it true, for my part,
>   See reasons and reasons ; this, to begin :
> 'Tis the faith that launched point-blank her dart
>   At the head of a lie—taught Original Sin,
> The Corruption of Man's Heart.

CHAPTER IX

SALVATION: THE CHRISTIAN REMEDY FOR SIN

A DEEP sense of the importance and the gravity of Sin is not peculiar to the Christian Religion ; it is found in many other systems. But Christianity is unique in the remedy for Sin which it proclaims,, and its doctrine of Salvation is supremely its " Gospel," or message of good news.

A.—MAN'S HELPLESSNESS AND THE SAVIOUR'S POWER

Sin has two aspects, and in either aspect man is helpless before it. (1) The sins of the past leave upon his conscience a burden of *guilt,* the distress of which will vary according to the individual constitution and temperament, but which may create an agony amounting almost to despair, as is seen in the case of John Bunyan. But in all ages the sense of guilt has haunted men, and they have asked, " Wherewith shall I come before the Lord, and bow myself before the high God ? . . . shall I give my firstborn for my transgression, the fruit of my body for the sin of my soul ?" (Micah vi. 6, 7). Sacrifices, pilgrimages, penances, men have tried them all under many different systems of religion ; yet, as was shown on pp. 73, 74, there is nothing that men can do for God, or give to Him, which can avail to atone for the past.

(2) Even if men were able to forget the past, however, every earnest soul realizes that he is sinful as well as guilty, and that Sin has terrible *power* over him. The more earnest his efforts to live a holy life, the more he recognizes that Sin has tainted his nature and entered into the secret springs of motive and desire. The classical passage on this subject is Rom. vii. It is not quite the truth to say that man is helpless against the power of evil habit, for resolute determination does enable him to conquer most external faults and vices, and, indeed, evil habits can never be mastered without earnest personal effort. But when this is done, evil motives and desires are still there ; a man cannot change his mind, his desires, or his inclinations, e.g., the mind may still be polluted though the actual life is chaste.

Christianity is unique in its proclamation of a personal Saviour who can deliver men from Sin in both its aspects.

(1) Over against the *guilt* of Sin it sets the atoning merits of the *Death* of Christ ; and (2) over against the *power* of sinful habit and desire it sets the present work and active help of the risen *Life* of Christ. See Rom. v. 10, and compare the lines:

> Be of sin the *double* cure,
> Save from wrath and make me pure.

B.—UNIVERSAL REDEMPTION, OR SALVATION FOR ALL

There is no disposition to deny that all men *need* salvation, for " all have sinned " (see Rom. iii. 23). But one of the historic controversies of Christianity has been over the question, *Can all men be saved?*

Arminianism and Calvinism. The Evangelical Churches, notably the Methodist, which maintain that God's mercy is free to all who will accept it by faith, are known as *Arminian,* that is, followers of a Dutch theologian called Arminius, who lived from 1560 to 1609. The chief leader on the other side was John Calvin of Geneva (1509-1564) ; and his followers are accordingly known as *Calvinists.* In Britain they have been found in the Presbyterian Churches of Scotland and among the older and stricter Baptists and Independents ; and traces of Calvinism are also to be seen in the Thirty-nine Articles of the Church of England. In its more extreme form this doctrine has now almost entirely disappeared, and modern Calvinists are often distinguished only by an earnest insistence on the Sovereignty of God, which is a wholesome corrective to light views of Sin and its importance. The more extreme doctrines of Calvinism may be stated thus:

(1) God is absolutely Sovereign, so much so that Man's will is not really free.

(2) As Sovereign Creator, God has the right to save some and reject others, and does actually do so by an eternal Election and Predestination.

(3) Man can neither help nor hinder this purpose of salvation or reprobation fixed by God's decrees.

The system is severely logical ; yet the manifest injustice of its conclusion is so repulsive that we feel instinctively that it cannot be true.

On two important points the two systems are in agreement: (1) In both salvation is by *grace,* i.e., the absolutely free, undeserved, mercy of God (Eph. ii. 8). (2) Both systems recognize that man cannot save himself: salvation is " not of works " (Eph. ii. 9), but by *faith,* and even that faith is the gift of God (Eph. ii. 8).

The two great points of difference are that— (1) The Arminians claim that man has a *part* in his own salvation, for it is the result of the working both of God and of the man himself. "Work out your own salvation with fear and trembling, for it is God which worketh in you "

(Phil. ii. 12, 13). (2) The Arminians claim that God's purpose of love and mercy extends to *all,* and that the merits of Christ's Death avail for all who are willing to claim them. The following passages may be noted:

" Who willeth that all men should be saved " (1 Tim. ii. 4).

" That by the grace of God He should taste death for every man " (Heb. ii. 9).

" That whosoever believeth on Him should not perish, but have eternal life " (John iii. 16).

" And he that is athirst, let him come : he that will, let him take the water of life freely " (Rev. xxii. 17).

Over against these we have to set a few passages which, at first sight appear to favour the Calvinist view, especially Rom. viii. 28-30 and ix. 1 - 24. Such passages receive detailed treatment in the commentaries, and must be studied there. But the following general considerations will remove most of the difficulties:

(1) *Calling* and *called*. These words may be rendered *invitation* and *invited*. They do not mean that some are called and others are not called ; but that the message of Salvation comes to all in the form of a gracious invitation from God.

(2) The words *Chosen* and *Elect* often correspond to our word *select,* as when we speak of a " select " or " choice " variety. " An elect race " (1 Peter ii. 9) means simply a choice race, one of special quality.

(3) The *predestination* of Rom. viii. 28 - 30 does not imply that God has predestined some to be saved and others to be lost. St. Paul is merely emphasizing the fact that behind any man's salvation there is a great age-long, purpose of God ; and that our salvation is a very sacred and solemn thing because it has been the hope and purpose of God from all eternity. He does not consider here the case of the unsaved ; but he would have said that they, too, were predestined to salvation, and that God had the same hope and purpose concerning them, though they have frustrated it. A mother may " predestine " her child for the ministry ; but, seeing that he has a will of his own, he may end upon the gallows !

(4) *Election*. Such a passage as, " Jacob I loved, but Esau I hated " (Rom. ix. 13), would not have been so strongly worded if it had been spoken originally in English. But harsh as it sounds, it makes no reference to salvation. It is simply the statement that God chose one brother rather than the other to fill a certain place in the world and to be the channel of His revelation to mankind. He gave Jacob the higher work, Esau the lower. The election was not to salvation, but to certain *privileges* and opportunities of *service* here. That some are in this way more highly privileged than others is an obvious fact of life ; but that does not mean that they have any greater chance of final salvation.

C.—THE CONDITIONS OF SALVATION

The Christian doctrine of Salvation is very fully illustrated by narratives of conversion in the Book of the Acts, such as the stories of the multitude at Pentecost (ii. 37-42), the Ethiopian eunuch (viii. 26-39), St. Paul (ix. 1-20), and the Philippian jailor (xvi. 25-34).

The Conditions of Salvation are generally said to be two: Repentance and Faith (Acts ii. 38 and xvi. 31); but to these we ought to add Confession (Rom. x. 9, 10) and Perseverance (Matt. xxiv. 13).

1, *Repentance*

Repentance is a change of mind, or change of will, and our word means a turning back or turning round. It has been defined as " Sorrow for sin with sincere purpose to forsake it." It is clearly a fundamental and necessary condition of salvation, for (1) it would not be right for God to *forgive* men, i.e., save them from the *guilt* of sin, without penitence on their part ; (2) it is impossible that even God should *cleanse* men from sin, i.e., save them from its *power*, unless they are willing to forsake it.

We can distinguish four elements which enter into a true repentance, and it will be seen that it is no light and easy experience. (1) The *sorrow* must be more than mere regret that one has acted foolishly, or that sin does not pay ; it must be more than sorrow that one has injured

others ; it must be " godly sorrow " (2 Cor. vii. 10),
i.e., sorrow for sin as sin against God, and sorrow for its
sinfulness rather than for its penalties. (2) It must manifest itself in *confession to God* (1 John i. 8, 9), i.e., the
acknowledgment of the sin of one's own deed and one's
own fault. (3) In the case of wrongs done to others it
must include confession to them and, if possible, *reparation,* e.g., by the restoration of stolen property. Such
reparation is never possible towards God. (4) It must
include a complete and final *break with sin,* at whatever
cost, and resolute personal effort to amend the life.

Repentance occupies an important place in the Old
Testament as well as in the New (see Psa. li. 17 ; Ezek.
xviii. 27 ; and Joel ii. 13).

Its Source. Multitudes feel no such penitence, for conviction of sin is the work of the Holy Spirit (John xvi. 8)
and not a natural human instinct. Christ is exalted " a
Prince and a Saviour, for to give repentance to Israel, and
remission of sins " (Acts v. 31). Hence the spirit of
penitence is a grace to be sought by prayer.

2. *Faith*

Our English word *faith* is, unfortunately, ambiguous,
and we use the same term both for belief in a statement,
for trust in a person, and for trustworthiness, e.g., " good
faith." We have also to distinguish between two kinds
of religious faith. *General Faith* is such a belief in God
and His Truth as inspired the lives of Abraham and the
other heroes named in Heb. xi. *Saving Faith* has been
well defined as " Such trust in Christ as leads us to rely
on Him alone as our Saviour, and to obey Him in all
things."

Saving Faith is thus much more than the acceptance of
a creed. In includes: (1) A belief that Christ *can* save,
both from the guilt of sin by His atoning merit, and from
the power of sin by His present help. (2) A belief that
Christ *is willing* to save. (3) An act of trust whereby we
commit ourselves to Him to be saved, precisely as a patient
puts himself in the hands of a doctor. (4) An act of trust

by which we undertake to *obey* Him. Just as a doctor can do little for a patient who will not follow his directions, Christ can do little for those who will not obey Him. Such obedience is rightly included under faith, for it is trust in the goodness and wisdom of Christ's will for us manifesting itself in practice. (5) Lastly, Saving Faith culminates in the simple belief that Christ *actually does save* us according to His promise.

St. Paul describes the inner working of this Faith in Rom. vi. 1-14. (1) Faith in the Death of Christ amounts to a *dying with Christ,* i.e., we acknowledge with Him that Sin is rightly punished, and adopt as our own His purpose to make propitiation for it. And it is also a *dying to Sin,* i.e., a complete repudiation of Sin and its claims upon us (cf. also Gal. vi. 14). (2) Faith in the Resurrection of Christ is to identify ourselves with His *new life,* and to claim the same power that wrought in Him to raise Him from the dead to work in us and re-create us in holiness.

3.   *Confession of Christ*

It is clear that in New Testament times some kind of *public profession of faith* in Christ was regarded as essential to salvation (see Rom. x. 9, and perhaps 1 John iv. 15). This confession usually took the form of Baptism (see Acts ii. 41, viii. 36, ix. 18, etc.), and, in the case of such a man as St. Paul, it was followed by preaching. The modern equivalents for it vary. In the case of those Churches which hold the principle of Adult Baptism, and in the case of converts from heathenism in all the Churches, the confession is still made by public Baptism. In the Anglican Church Confirmation, and in some other Churches public recognition as a member of the Church, has this for its main purpose ; whilst very often the confession is made in a testimony meeting. In any case there is also required the confession of an upright life.

4.   *Perseverance*

The New Testament lays much stress on the need of Perseverance, and contains many warnings against the danger of backsliding and lapsing from the Faith (see

Mark xiii. 13 ; John xv. 6 ; 1 Thess. v 19 ; 2 Tim. ii. 12 ; Heb. x. 23). Some have held that a man once saved is always saved, and bring forward the words of Jesus, " No one shall snatch them out of My hand " (John x. 28, 29). But this saying means only that the power of Christ is sufficient to protect the believer against all foes so long as he is willing to continue in the fold ; it does not mean that it is impossible for him to wander from the fold. Instances like that of Demas (2 Tim. iv. 10), St. Paul's fear lest he himself should finally " be rejected " (1 Cor. ix. 27), and the terrible words of Heb. vi. 4-6 and x. 26, 27, serve as a continual warning to the best.

It should be noted with regard to these Conditions of Salvation that they are remarkably *simple* and *universally possible*. They are probably the only conditions capable of fulfilment by old and young, rich and poor, learned and ignorant in every land ; and they should be contrasted with other conditions which have sometimes been laid down, e.g., knowledge, pilgrimages and offerings. They appear to be the only conditions possible in a universal religion, and are one more proof that Christianity is a religion for the whole race.

D.—MAN'S EXPERIENCE OF SALVATION

We may now consider the subject of Salvation as it comes to men in experience, and examine the various stages through which the believer passes.

1. *The Change in God's Attitude*

As was explained on page 37, God's attitude towards the sinner personally is always one of love ; but, in so far as a man identifies himself with sin, he is alienated from God, and God's attitude towards him is described as one of " wrath " (John iii. 36 ; Rom. i. 18). Three terms are used to express the change that takes place in this attitude.

The word *Pardon* is used when God is regarded as Sovereign ; for pardon is the passing over of offences against authority, and only the Law-giver or Sovereign has the power and the right to grant it.

The word *Forgiveness* is used when God is regarded as the injured party. Any man who has been wronged can forgive the injury, and God's forgiveness is the passing over of offences in so far as they are offences against Himself.

The very important word *Justification* belongs peculiarly to Christianity. To justify a sinner is more than to pardon or forgive him: it is to treat him as if he were righteous, and reinstate him as if the offence had never been. The employer who abstains from prosecuting a defaulting clerk may be said to " forgive him." But to " justify " him would mean to treat the lapse as if it had never occurred, and reinstate the man in his employment.

Justification is the result of *faith* in the atoning merit of Christ. The propitiation made by Him is *imputed* or reckoned to the credit of the believer, and for the sake of that he is treated as if he himself were righteous. St. Paul in Phil. iii. 9 contrasts " the righteousness of the law," i.e., the righteousness which would belong to the man who perfectly obeyed the law, with " the righteousness which is of God by faith," i.e., the righteousness imputed to those who trust in the merits of Christ. On the whole subject see Rom. iv. 1-8.

It is worth while to *ask what are the results of Forgiveness and Justification?*

(1) What Forgiveness does *not* do:

(*a*) The actual deeds of the past remain: they are facts and cannot be unmade, for they have entered into the history of the Universe. So far the haunting lines of Omar Khayyam are true:

> The Moving Finger writes ; and having writ
> Moves on : nor all your Piety nor Wit
> Shall lure it back to cancel half a Line,
> Nor all your Tears wash out a Word of it.

(*b*) The natural consequences of our sins remain. If a man has wrecked his constitution and his fortune by dissipation, Forgiveness does not restore to him either health or wealth, though these may be regained in course of time by temperance and industry. In the same way, Forgiveness does not annul the sorrowful consequences that a man's sins may bring to his family and friends.

(c) The consequences of sin in a man's disposition remain. Forgiveness does not destroy the drunkard's craving, though that may be broken by the sanctifying grace of God mentioned in the next section.

(d) The sorrowful remembrance of sin remains, and gives a tinge of melancholy to life ever afterwards. Cf. St. Paul's undying remorse for the days when he had been a "blasphemer, and a persecutor, and injurious" (1 Tim. i. 13).

(2) What Forgiveness *does* do:

(a) The punishment of sin, and especially the future punishment of sin, as distinct from its natural consequences, is cancelled.

(b) The guilt of sin is cancelled, and the barrier between the soul and God is removed ; and this is incomparably the most important outcome of Forgiveness. "There is therefore now *no condemnation* to them that are in Christ Jesus" (Rom. viii. 1, cf. 33). In Rom. v. 1 the result is described as "*peace* with God."

2. *The Change in the Penitent's Nature*

The word *Conversion* is used to represent the whole process of Salvation apart from subsequent growth and sanctification. More strictly it means the turning about from sin to righteousness. Its importance is that it lays stress on the reality of the change that takes place in the nature of the man. Justification may appear to have a somewhat unreal and fictitious character, and has been irreverently described as a pretending that a man is righteous when he is not really so. But side by side with Justification, i.e., treating as holy, there is a real change or process of *Sanctification,* i.e., making holy, as the result of which the man may rightly be treated as innocent now, even though he has sinned in the past.

The terms *New Birth* and *Regeneration* are used to

describe this change. Such a change of heart is prayed for in Psa. li. 10, and is promised in Jer. xxxi. 33 and Ezek. xxxvi. 25, 26. The phrase New Birth is taken from our Lord's discourse with Nicodemus in John iii. 1 - 15. Note also the text, " If any man is in Christ he is *a new creature* (or, there is a new *creation*): the old things are passed away ; behold, they are become new " (2 Cor. v. 17). This doctrine indicates: (1) that with Conversion a man may make a new beginning ; (2) that there is a real change in the heart ; (3) that he enters into a new spiritual world ; (4) that at first he is a "babe in Christ," and has therefore to grow and develop in the Christian life.

The secret of this change of heart is found in the active righteousness of Christ which is *imparted* to the believer and implanted in him (see 1 Cor. i. 30 and 2 Cor. v. 21). Distinguish carefully *Justification* by which a man is *counted holy* as the result of the *imputed* merit of Christ, from *Regeneration* and *Sanctification* by which a man is *made holy* as the result of the *imparted* righteousness of Christ.

3. *The New Relationship to God*

The word *Adoption* is used to indicate the fact that the forgiven penitent becomes in a special sense the child of God (see John i. 12, 13 ; Rom. viii. 14 - 17, and Gal, iv. 5, 6). Men are by nature children of the Heavenly Father ; but the Adoption of believers means that they enter into conscious spiritual sonship, and are restored to those privileges of sonship which they had forfeited.

4. *The Assurance of Salvation*

It is the teaching of the New Testament that a man may *know* that he is a child of God, and that the fact is *witnessed to him by the Spirit* in his heart (Rom. viii. 16). This experience varies greatly in its distinctness ; but it is meant to be the privilege of all believers, though all do not attain it. Its absence does not necessarily indicate that a man is unsaved. Many who are in perfect health are haunted by morbid fears of disease. If such a man chances to meet a doctor who can inspire sufficient confidence his fears may be dissipated in a moment, and he will enter into the conscious enjoyment of health. The absence of the joyous assurance of salvation is usually the result of unwillingness to believe that Christ has actually done that which He has promised, or unwillingness to trust and to cling to those assurances of acceptance which come at times even to the most despondent believer.

E.—THE NEW LIFE IN CHRIST

1. *Union with Christ*

The new life of the believer is a life " hid with Christ in God " (Col. iii. 3). That is to say, it consists in the actual life of Christ in the heart through His Spirit (Gal. ii. 20), so that it may be said that Christ *is* our life (Col. iii. 4). In John vi. 48-58 Christ describes Himself as the Living Bread, but this idea of union with Himself is most fully developed in the Parable of the Vine (John xv. 1-10). The outcome of such a union is seen in the list of the fruits of the Spirits (Gal. v. 22), in which the graces of the Christian character are represented as the natural result of the Divine life in the soul.

2. *Temptation and the Tempter*

Many figures such as the race and the warfare are used to show that the present life is one of effort and of discipline. The chief perils of the soul are summed up in the word *Temptation*. The new Testament teaches that Temptation does not come from God (James i. 13), but is sometimes permitted by Him as an inevitable part of human experience in which Jesus Himself shared (Heb. ii. 18, iv. 15). In such cases it serves the purpose of moral education and discipline (James i. 2, 3, 12) ; and there comes with the temptation grace sufficient to resist it (1 Cor. x 13).

The *origin of temptation* is explained in two ways:

(1) James i. 14, 15 speaks of *lusts* or evil desires which remain in the soul, subdued but not destroyed. When these meet with any external enticement or opportunity they produce sin.

(2) More frequently temptation is described as the deliberate and malicious suggestion of the great spirit of evil—the *Devil* or *Satan* (Matt. iv. 1-11). The personal existence of such a prince of evil has been much disputed, and many contend that the name is only a personification in thought, by which we sum up the evil influences that exist around us. The chief *objection* urged against belief in his existence is that it implies two rival and almost omnipotent rulers in the Universe. But this conception of Satan is probably derived from Milton's majestic portrait of him rather than from the Bible.

(a) According to the Bible Satan is neither eternal nor uncreated. In Job i. he is described as in some sense a servant of God. In Gen. iii., where he appears in the guise of the serpent, he is represented as cunning and malicious rather than great. In the New Testament he is described as a spiritual being who has revolted from God and who is the active enemy of the soul (1 Peter v. 8) and the great opponent of the kingdom of God (Matt. xiii. 38, 39 and Eph. vi. 12).

(b) He is not represented in the Bible as omnipotent ; and, though as a spiritual being, he is described as intensely active, he is not omnipresent, for Jesus speaks of him as coming, not as present with Him (John xiv. 30).

(c) His rivalry to God is not to be eternal and in the end he will be overthrown (Rev. xx. 2, 3, 10).

There are important *reasons for retaining the belief in his real existence*.

(i) Jesus repeatedly speaks of him as a person. It is suggested that in doing so He accommodated His language to the current ideas of the people, just as a mother speaks to her child in language which is not strictly accurate, but which the child will understand. It is possible that in some matters Jesus did this, and there were certainly some things which He withheld because His disciples were not ready to hear them (John xvi. 12). But it is incredible that He would have allowed them to continue in error on a matter of such great spiritual importance as this.

(ii) Many temptations seem to come to us by direct malicious suggestion from without.

(iii) The experience of Christian workers, the infinite variety of the forms of evil, and the baffling way in which after being checked at one point it reappears at another, all suggest the existence of some great, hidden, organizing genius of evil and mastermind of sin. For this see Eph. vi. 12.

3. *Christian Perfection*

The ideal and goal of the Christian life is known as *Christian Perfection,* and is well described in such a passage as James i. 4, where the word " perfect " (*teleios*) points to full, mature growth, and the word " entire " (*holocleros*) indicates a completeness of character in which no grace is missing.

Christian Perfection has two aspects: (1) As regards the *will* of the believer, it is the solemn devotion of one's whole being to God and the purpose to abstain completely from every known sin. In this aspect it is called *Entire Sanctification*. (2) As regards the *heart* and the *emotions,* it consists of wholehearted love to God combined with the experience of God's perfect love shed abroad in the heart. It is then described as *Perfect Love.*

The term perfection is liable to misunderstanding, and it is safer always to speak of this grace as *Christian* Perfection. It is distinguished from absolute perfection in many ways, and the prejudice that is sometimes felt against the doctrine would disappear if this were generally understood.

(1) It is not *faultless* though it is *sinless*. That is to say, a man may have many defects of mind, temperament and judgment, which lead him to act foolishly or awkwardly. These are faults, and prevent him from being an ideal man ; but, inasmuch as they are constitutional defects for which he is not responsible, they are not sins.

(2) It does not involve exemption from all *temptation,* for even the Saviour was tempted. But the temptations will now come by prompting from without, rather than from evil inclination within.

(3) It does not enable a man to dispense with the prayer for *forgiveness*. The life of the holiest of men to-day is poorer, and his service is less effective than it might have been, in consequence of the sin of his earlier days. Further, there are always sins and shortcomings of the community and the Church, for which each one has some responsibility.

(4) It does not preclude *growth and moral development*. The hand of a boy of ten may be perfect for his age (*holocleros*), but it will have to grow in size and strength and skill if it is still to be a perfect (*teleios*) hand when he is twenty. The whole capacity to love and serve God should increase with the passing of the years ; so that, if there is not corresponding growth in love and in grace, the perfection of to-day will not be perfection in five years' time.

Christian Perfection is set forth both as a *possibility* and as a *duty* in many promises and exhortations of the New Testament (see Matt. xxii. 37 ; Rom. vi. 12-14 ; 2 Cor. vii. 1 ; 1 John iii. 6). It cannot, therefore, be regarded merely as a vague ideal, never meant to be realised.

A close study of St. Paul's description of his own experience in Phil. iii. 12-16 indicates that there are three stages in its realization.

(1) *Perfect*. In a certain sense he is willing to use the word " perfect " concerning himself and others in the Philippian Church (*v.* 15). This lower perfection appears to consist in the fact that he is now trying to " apprehend " (or, lay hold of) that for which Christ had " apprehended " (or, laid hold of) him. The change may be compared to the case of a little child who was formerly content with things on his own familiar level, but now feels himself laid hold of and lifted up by his father, and accordingly becomes eager to lay hold of things on that higher level, which were before beyond his reach and probably outside even his thought. St. Paul at this stage has recognized, as the average believer does not do at conversion, that it is Christ's purpose to give him complete dominion over sin, from moment to moment ; and he has made that

purpose his own, daring to look for its fulfilment through continual dependence on Christ by faith.   This is certainly a distinct stage of experience, and, inasmuch as perfection has now become a definite aim and a confident expectation, it may be called a stage of Christian Perfection.

(2) *Pressing on.*   What has just been described represents a definitely and permanently higher experience.   Yet it is only a partial perfection: the actual realization of all the possibilities of this higher life is only gradual and almost always defective.   The Christian finds that there are unexpected heights and depts of love, and virtues and graces of character of which he was formerly ignorant, but which he now desires.   And so St. Paul describes an experience of struggle and effort—he has not yet " obtained," and is not yet " made perfect," i.e., the work of perfecting is not yet completed.   The life of the Christian ministry furnishes a parallel.   A young man is conscious of entering on a distinctly new phase of life when he is received into the ministry: an ambition has been realized, and in some sense he has attained his goal.   But, having attained so far, he becomes increasingly conscious of what is involved in being a minister, and probably realizes increasingly his own shortcomings.   He is in the ministry, but feels himself a long way from being a minister in the highest sense of the term.   So St. Paul, though he was in some sense " perfect," felt that he was not yet " made perfect " or " perfected."

(3) *Made perfect.*   The last stage of really perfected love and finished character is the hope which is our continual inspiration ; but probably none can ever be sure of reaching it until eternity.

CHAPTER X

THE CHURCH AND THE MINISTRY

THE Church, the Ministry, and the Sacraments stand for the material, the earthly, and the practical side of the Christian Religion. Now it is notorious that men may agree in their principles and ideals, and yet differ greatly as to how they ought to be carried into effect, e.g., those who are eager for social reform are far from agreeing in their practical schemes of reform. Hence we shall find that the most numerous and the most lasting controversies of Christianity are not those connected with doctrine, but those connected with the Church and the Ministry. For in practical matters every man feels himself competent to form a judgment, and in connexion with the organization and worship of the Church all the conflicting tastes and prejudices of men enter into the discussion.

A.—THE CHURCH

1. *The need for the Church.* The Church has arisen to meet the *social instinct* found in man. Life in its fulness cannot be lived in isolation ; and the same instinct that brings men together in societies, cities and states has led the followers of Christ to unite in a Christian community or society, the Church.

The phrase *the Communion of Saints* is used to describe the religious form of this social instinct. The Parable of the Vine reminds us that Christian believers have a living connexion with one another, for the common life of Christ enters into all. The natural result is mutual interest and the desire to help one another. The impulse to pray for distant missionary workers is one illustration of this principle ; and the fact that such prayers avail to help them is a proof that this united life in Christ is a reality. But the Church also believes that the Communion of Saints embraces even the sainted and glorified dead, for all are one in Christ.

130

The Value of the Church. Men have gained in at least three ways by coming together in communities: (1) They have secured protection against their common foes. (2) The combined life has meant greater wealth: where some plough and some build and some hunt and some make clothes, the average of wealth is greater than where each individual has to try to carry on all these different kinds of work for himself. (3) Human society is a mental and moral stimulus ; and in a large town to-day it is possible to provide libraries, concerts, entertainments and meetings, which are quite impossible in a small village.

It sometimes appears that the modern highly organized and costly Church is a strange development from the informal work of Jesus of Nazareth ; but its development has been as natural and inevitable as the growth of the modern city or state. The Church has grown into what it is (1) to provide mutual protection and help against the forces of evil ; (2) to provide a fuller and richer religious life through mutual encouragement, instruction, and prayer ; (3) to create the great enterprises of Home and Foreign Missions, which are possible only by the united efforts of the many.

2. *Definitions and Distinctions.* The word *Church* is particularly ambiguous. It is used in the following senses: (1) A sacred building. (2) The company worshipping there. (3) A union of such companies of believers, e.g., "The Methodist Church." (4) The whole number of known believers now living, e.g., "The Christian Church of to-day." (5) The whole body of such believers, past, present, and to come.

The difference may be illustrated by two typical definitions of the Church. The first follows the lines of (2) above:

"A Church is a company of professed believers, in which the Word of God is faithfully preached, and the Sacraments are duly administered."

The second follows the lines of (4) above:

"The Church of Christ is the visible communion founded

by Him, consisting of all who confess the faith of Christ, and are united in the worship of God, in His service, and in fellowship with one another.''

The following distinctions should be noted:

The Church and *The Churches*.   The congregation worshipping at the City Temple is *a* Church, and the Church of England is *a* Church ; but the whole body of Christian believers is *the* Church.

The *Visible* Church consists of those now living who are recognized as avowed followers of Christ ; the Church *Invisible* includes the sainted dead, and also the unrecognized followers of Christ, of whom there may be great numbers.

The Church *Militant* is the Church now on earth, fighting its battles against the world and sin.   The Church *Triumphant* consists of those who have accomplished their warfare.

The *Kingdom of God* includes everything and everyone that is touched for good by the influence of Christianity, and everyone who is eventually to acknowledge God's sovereignty.   The *Church* (*Militant*) corresponds to the fighting army which is winning that kingdom for God.

3.   *The Church in the Teaching of Jesus*.   It can hardly be denied that it was the purpose of Jesus that His disciples should continue as a distinct society after His Ascension. The idea of the Kingdom of Heaven which entered so largely into His teaching indicates this, for a kingdom is a community, not a number of isolated individuals.

With regard to the Church, as He instituted it, we may note that: (1) The basis of membership and bond of union between its members was to be the *Confession of faith* in Himself.   This is clearly indicated in the difficult passage, Matt. xvi. 15-18, which is discussed more fully on pp. 144-5.

(2) New members were to be introduced into the community by the ceremony of *Baptism* (Matt. xxviii. 19).

(3) The Church was entrusted with a great *Commission*, to propagate the Gospel and gather all nations into the Kingdom (Matt. xxviii. 19, 20).

The words, "If he refuse to hear the Church" (Matt. xviii. 17), indicate that the Church has a right to speak with *authority* in disputes between its members. Much more remarkable is the power of *binding and loosing* granted to His followers in the words, "What things soever ye shall bind on earth shall be bound in heaven: and what things soever ye shall loose on earth shall be loosed in heaven" (Matt. xviii. 18). The word *bind* is here equivalent to forbid, and the word *loose* to allow. The meaning is not that the Church is strictly infallible in its judgment on matters either of doctrine or of conduct ; but that the decision of a united body of Christian people, arrived at by careful thought and prayer, must be taken as correct for practical purposes, and becomes a standard which the individual ought to respect, seeing that it is recognized in Heaven as the correct standard under the circumstances. The judgment of good parents is not always infallible. But when they have reached their decision thoughtfully and prayerfully, it becomes a standard for their child which will be recognized in Heaven : what they bind, or forbid, is bound, or forbidden, in the judgment of Heaven ; and what they loose, or allow, is loosed, or allowed, in the judgment of Heaven (cf. Eph. vi. 1).

4. *The Church in the Acts.* The stories of conversion in the Acts make two points clear: (1) The immediate sequel of conversion was to join the Church ; so much so that the conversion of a large number is described by the words, "The Lord added to them day by day those that were being saved" (Acts ii. 47). (2) In accordance with the teaching of Jesus, admission to the Church was in every case by *Baptism*.

The *united life* of the Apostolic Church is described in Acts ii. 42: "And they continued stedfastly in the apostles' teaching and (in) fellowship, in the breaking of bread and the prayers." We thus find four characteristics : (1) A common doctrine—the Apostles' teaching. (2) The breaking of bread, or Lord's Supper. (3) United public worship at stated times—" *the* prayers." (4) Fellowship.

The meaning of the word *fellowship* is a little difficult to determine ; and it is not certain whether in this passage we should read " in the apostles' fellowship," or simply " in fellowship," i.e., with one another. 1 John i. 7 speaks of " fellowship one with another," but 1 John i. 3 says emphatically that " our fellowship is with the Father and with His Son Jesus Christ." So that it would appear that the Christian has, in the first instance, fellowship with God, and that the natural result of this should be fellowship with his brother Christians. The strict meaning of the word is a *sharing* or *partnership,* and the case is met when there is a spirit of *comradeship* between the members of the Church. To feel an interest in the enterprises of the Church and contribute towards them is a kind of fellowship ; to take a direct part in its spiritual work, e.g., as a Sunday-school teacher, is certainly to act as a real partner. But there is still room for the expression of fellowship, or comradeship, between the members of the Church. The Methodist Church makes a unique, and very successful, attempt to provide for this by means of the Class Meeting, in which a number of members are grouped together to help one another by free and informal conversation on the difficulties of the religious life, and by prayer for one another.

There is also a reference in Acts ii. 44, 45, to a modified *Communism.* It appears to have been only an experiment, and did not last long. In any case, it was not what a modern Socialist understands by community of goods, for the property was not pooled, and then divided: each man's possessions remained at his own disposal (Acts v. 4), but were regarded as available for others, by his consent, when they had *need* (Acts iv. 35). The permanent result of this was simply a special concern for the poor of the Church (Gal. vi. 10).

Early Organization. As converts were made in new neighbourhoods suitable officers were appointed (Acts xiv. 23); and in most ways the Churches so formed appear to have been independent. Yet all recognized the authority of the Apostles ; and the Council at Jerusalem (Acts xv. 1-29), which was the first great gathering of delegates from the various Churches, came to decisions which were accepted as binding on all.

5. *The Church in the Epistles and the Revelation.* The separate congregations are still regarded as independent Churches, cf. the seven Churches of Asia in Rev. i. 11. Yet there is a union between them: the missionary Churches unite in the collection for the poor saints at Jerusalem (see 2 Cor. viii. 1-5), and St. Paul is at pains to show that his work is in harmony with that of the other Apostles (see Gal. ii. 6-10).

At the same time we see gradually emerging in the teaching of St. Paul the idea of a great, invisible, spiritual entity—*the* Church. This embraces all the local Churches and more, for it includes the saints that have been and those that are yet to be. Three important figures are used to describe it.

(1) In 1 Cor, iii. 16, and especially in Eph. ii. 21, 22, the Church is described as the *Temple* of God, the special home and dwelling-place of the Holy Spirit. This does not restrict the working of the Spirit to the visible Church ; but it does indicate that He dwells in a peculiar sense among the avowed followers of Christ, and works most freely through them.

(2) Throughout 1 Cor. xii. and in Eph. iv. 11-16 the Church is represented as the *Body* of which Christ is the *Head,* the various branches of the Church or the individual believers corresponding to the parts of the Body. It is from this figure that we derive our term "Church-member," for the original meaning of the word *member* was a limb, or part of the body. Three important truths are taught by this analogy: (a) That there is a living union between Christ and all true members of His Church, similar to that between the head and the parts of the body : (b) that there is a living connexion between all true members, so that each needs the others, as is the case with the various parts of the body ; (c) that, just as a man expresses himself to others and executes his will by means

of his body, so the Church is the great instrument by which Christ utters His message to men and executes His purposes in the world.

(3) In Eph. v. 25-27, and frequently in the Book of the Revelation, the Church is described as the *Bride* of Christ. This indicates that she is the object of His special love, and almost that she is Christ's " other self," something needed to complete His Being (see Eph. v. 31, 32).

6. *Roman Catholicism and Protestantism.* The history of the Church since New Testament times has been one of rapid growth in numbers and influence and of great development in organization and enterprise. But it has also been a history of strife and division.

The first great division dated from as early as A.D. 451, when the Roman Empire had become really two empires— a Western part, mainly Latin-speaking, with Rome as its capital, and an Eastern portion, Greek-speaking, with Byzantium (i.e., Constantinople) as its capital. The division in the Church arose from jealousy between these two capitals. The West claimed that the Bishop of Rome (the " Pope ") was the earthly head of the Christian Church ; the East made the same claim for the " Patriarch " of Constantinople. Hence there arose the *Eastern Church* (or *Greek Church*) which is still found in Russia, Greece, Bulgaria and Eastern Europe generally, and the *Roman Catholic Church,* which we know in Western Europe. But much the most important of the cleavages has been that caused by the *Protestant Reformation* within the Roman Church.

The subject requires a separate volume for its treatment, but we may note here *the leading doctrines of Roman Catholicism* against which the Reformation was a protest. Some of these receive further notice later in this chapter.

(1) That the Pope, or Bishop of Rome, is the successor of St. Peter, the Vicar (or *substitute*) of Christ, the Head of the Church on earth, and infallible.

(2) That the Ministry is a sacrificing priesthood, and that the only valid Orders are those derived by direct succession from the Apostles.

(3) That in the Sacrament of the Lord's Supper there is a transformation or transubstantiation of the elements into the actual Body and Blood of Christ.

(4) That Aural Confession must be made to a Priest, who has the power to grant absolution.

(5) That the Virgin Mary is the mother of God, not merely the mother of the human nature of our Lord, and, therefore, worthy of worship.

(6) That the "Saints," in virtue of their "works of supererogation," i.e., works which exceed the demands of duty, have accumulated merit by which they can help men in answer to prayer.

(7) That the dead are in Purgatory, and that, therefore, it is right to pray for them.

(8) That the worship of images is permissible.

The Roman Church explains these extraordinary departures from the teaching of the New Testament by the assertion that the tradition of the Church is of, at least, equal authority with the Bible. In so far as the Bible is studied at all it must be interpreted by the Church, and the individual member has no right of private judgment.

7. *Modern Protestant Divisions*. The modern Church in Britain is divided into Anglican, Presbyterian, Methodist, Congregational, Baptist, and other Churches.

To some extent they are divided on questions of *doctrine*. The Presbyterians are Calvinistic ; the Methodists, evangelical or Arminian. The Anglicans, Presbyterians, and Methodists are bound by more or less definite statements of creed ; the Congregationalists, whilst they generally hold the orthodox belief, do not tie themselves to any precise statement of it. The Baptists are distinguished by their insistence on Adult Baptism and Baptism by Immersion.

There are more important differences of *Church Organization and Government*. The Anglican Church recognizes three orders in the Ministry: Bishops, Priests, and Deacons ; and the government of the Church and its spiritual work are almost entirely in the hands of the clergy. The Methodists and the Presbyterians give a large share to the laity, both in the government and in the spiritual work. The government of Congregational and Baptist Churches is by the Church Meeting of members.

The Anglican, Presbyterian, and Methodist Churches are *connexional* systems: that is, the various congregations unite to form one body, and, except in purely local matters, each congregation is under the authority of a central Assembly, such as the Methodist Conference, which has power to make laws binding on the whole Church. The Congregational and Baptist Churches are *independent,* and each congregation claims the right to govern itself without interference from outside. Their Councils and Unions meet for consultation, but have no power to legislate.

There are also considerable differences between the Churches in their forms of worship.

The existence of these divisions is in many ways regrettable, but it has some great compensations. No one system is found, in its entirety, in the New Testament, though each can claim that it preserves some valuable features of the Apostolic Church ; and under each system splendid service has been rendered to the Kingdom of God. So that, if any of these Churches will abstain from claiming exclusive possession of the truth, a good case can be made out for it on practical grounds ; it is an advantage that there should be Churches differing in worship and in government and in the doctrines that they emphasize, for in this way provision is made for the religious needs of men of all types and all temperaments.

8. *Catholicity and Schism.* The division of the Church has some deplorable aspects, and the Nonconformist Churches are charged by the Romanists and Anglicans with violating the *Unity* of Christ's Body. It is claimed that *Catholicity,* or world-wide unity, is an essential mark of the true Church ; see Christ's great prayer for unity in John xvii. The Nonconformist reply is that true Catholicity does not consist in uniformity of worship or of organization, but in universal sympathy and goodwill. A Church is truly catholic in so far as it recognizes all other Churches which are loyal to Christ as its

equals and as true parts of the one Church Catholic. The real breach of Catholicity occurs when one Church repudiates the others, and appropriates to itself the name of the Catholic Church. It is as false to call the Church of Rome the Catholic Church as to call the English people the human race. The name " Roman Catholic " is a contradiction in terms, for no one section of the Church can be the whole Church.

The name *Schism* is given by the High Church to what they describe as the " sin of division." It appears from the New Testament, however, that the word really stands for the spirit of faction, and strife within a Church, rather than for peaceable separation from that particular branch of the Church. There is a Schism in a home where several adults live together in a spirit of wrangling ; and the best way of ending such Schism and preserving the family unity may be for the various members of the household to set up separate establishments, in which they can live their lives in independence and with goodwill towards one another. In so far as the Nonconformist Churches bear goodwill to the Established Church, there is no Schism in their separation from it ; Schism might, and probably would, have arisen if they had remained within the Church discontented and at variance with it.

The two great New Testament figures for the Church are suggestive. If the Church is the Temple of God, we may conceive it as a noble cathedral, with nave, aisle, transepts and subsidiary chapels, each with its individual character and use, like the various branches of the Church, yet all combining to form one whole. Again, if the Church is the Body of Christ, we may expect it to have many different parts, each exercising its own functions, like the organs of the body, yet all combining to form one living whole.

The One-True-Church theory would lead to the cast-iron unity of an artificial *organization*. The unity aimed at by the independent, and yet friendly and co-operating Churches, is the unity of a living *organism* or body, in which the different parts are more or less separate and independent, but are all animated by the one life within.

B.—THE MINISTRY

1. *The Separated Ministry*. The existence of a Ministry which is separated to the work of the Gospel and has no other occupation, is justified by the following considerations:

(1) The Apostles and such men as Timothy and Titus appear to have been given wholly to the work of the Church.

(2) The words of Jesus in Luke x. 1-9, and of St. Paul in 1 Cor. ix. 1-1 4 and Gal. vi. 6, 7, give such workers a definite claim to maintenance at the expense of the Church. St. Paul also adds a claim for maintenance as a married man, if so desired ; and instances the case of St. Peter and others who were married. At the same time, St. Paul often preferred to maintain himself by his trade of tent-making—(a) because in the early days, when the Christian community was drawn largely from the slave population, his maintenance would have been an oppressive burden upon them ; and (b) because in the case of a Church like that at Corinth there were hostile members to whom he did not care to be indebted. But Phil. iv. 14-16 makes it clear that he accepted monetary help with thankfulness on more than one occasion from the friendly Church at Philippi.

(3) The work of the Church in modern days imperatively demands trained and expert workers, just as specialists are required in every other department of life.

The *qualifications* for a place in the Ministry are three : (1) Personal character, devotion, experience, and gifts (see Rom. xii. 6, 7 ; 1 Tim. iii. 1-6 ; 2 Tim. ii. 21 ; 1 Pet. iv. 10).

(2) The call of God. See John xv. 16 ; Acts xiii. 2 ; and St. Paul's continual references to his own call to preach (Rom. i. 1 ; 1 Cor. i. 1, etc.).

(3) The call of the Church. The call of God is inward and personal, and is liable to be misinterpreted. It must therefore be confirmed by the judgment of the Christian

community in which the man is known. For instance, even the deacons in Acts vi. 3 were to be selected by the Church.

The *work* of the Minister has three main divisions : (1) Preaching (cf. the great commission in Matt. xxviii. 19). (2) Tending the flock of God, or pastoral work (see John xxi. 15-17 ; Acts xx. 28-30). (3) The administration of the Sacraments. Probably no Nonconformist would maintain that the teaching of Scripture absolutely restricts this to the Ministry. But Baptism and the Lord's Supper occupy such an important place in the life of the Church that they are always entrusted to official representatives of the Church, and in most Churches to the Ministry only.

The ceremony by which Ministers are set apart is known as *Ordination*. Following the usage of the New Testament Church (see Acts xiii. 3 ; 2 Tim. i. 6), the distinctive feature of this service has always been the imposition of hands, i.e., the placing of their hands upon the head of the candidate either by senior ministers or by bishops.

2. *The Nonconformist View of the Ministry*. The Nonconformists hold that ordination has real results, and that the Minister is not merely a church-worker who happens to be paid. (1) It is fair to assume that in answer to the prayers of the Church *gifts and graces* suitable for his work are bestowed upon him. (2) Inasmuch as he becomes largely responsible for the control of the Church, the teaching of its doctrine, and the administration of its discipline, he must be granted a suitable measure of *authority* by the Church.

But Nonconformists do not admit that there is any essential difference between the Ministry and the devout Laity.

(1) The Minister is not a priest, except as all believers are priests.

(2) The Ministry has not a monopoly of the Spirit and His gifts. The tongues of fire at Pentecost sat upon *each* of them, including the women (Acts ii. 3) ; and the rank and file of the members of the Corinthian Church were

endowed with striking spiritual gifts (see 1 Cor. xii. 4-11 and 28-30).

(3) The Ministry has not a monopoly of the spiritual work of the Church. Accordingly the members of the Church take a large share in its work as lay preachers, etc. In most of the Churches the administration of the Sacraments is confined somewhat strictly to the Ministry, not in the belief that they would be invalid if administered by laymen, but as a matter of Church order and to give a specially solemn character to these unique services.

3. *The High Church View of the Ministry.* There are very serious differences between the view of the Ministry held by Nonconformists and Evangelical Churchmen, and that held by the High Anglicans and Roman Catholics.

(1) *Ordination.* The High Church claims that Ordination literally sets men in *a class apart,* so much so that the Sacraments are valid when administered by an ungodly clergyman, but invalid when administered by a godly layman. Until comparatively recently a clergyman of the Church of England was regarded as " once in Orders always in Orders " ; and could neither resign them nor be deprived of them, even though he were an unbeliever, a drunkard, a rake, or a thief. He could, however, be debarred from exercising clerical functions.

(2) *The Three Orders.* The High Church also recognizes *three orders* in the Ministry: (*a*) *Deacons,* who are, in some sense, Ministers on trial, or Probationers ; (*b*) *Priests,* who are permitted to administer the Sacraments ; and (*c*) *Bishops,* who alone can ordain to the Ministry.

Nonconformity does not deny that this has proved itself a good working system. But it does deny that it is laid down in the New Testament or binding upon the Christian Church ; for the New Testament recognizes no sacrificing Priesthood, and only one order of Ministers.

(*a*) The *Deacons of Acts* vi. 1-6 correspond to Churchwardens or Stewards rather than to Ministers, for they had to do chiefly with Church finance.

(*b*) The New Testament speaks frequently of two classes

of officials—*Elders* and *Bishops*. Some, instead of translating the former word, use the Greek word with an English spelling, and speak of *Presbyters*. But it is admitted by such great Anglican scholars as Bishop Lightfoot that the Elders (or Presbyters) and the Bishops were the same, and that either name could be used for them. Hence there is no three-fold Ministry in the New Testament: it recognizes only Deacons, who were hardly Ministers at all, and Ministers proper, who were called sometimes Elders (or Presbyters) and sometimes Bishops. There is thus really only one order in the Ministry.

(*c*) The word *Priest* perhaps came into English by a slurring of the word Presbyter in pronunciation. But it is also used to translate an entirely different Greek word (*hiereus*), which is never employed in the New Testament to describe the Christian Ministry. Yet it is in this sense of "sacrificing priest" that the Roman Catholics and Anglicans use it.

(*d*) The word *Bishop* means simply an *overseer* or *superintendent,* and the New Testament Elders were called by this name when this aspect of their work was to the front. Hence the title Bishop is rightly given in the Methodist Episcopal Church of the United States to those ministers whose work is the general supervision of the Churches ; for they do not claim to differ essentially from their brother ministers, as an Anglican Bishop does, but are merely chosen for the work of supervision. In the same way the Superintendent Minister of a Methodist Circuit corresponds to a New Testament Bishop.

(3) *Priesthood.* The High Anglican or the Romanist Priest claims to offer a *sacrifice* in the Sacrament of the Lord's Supper, or the Mass ; and all Roman Catholic and many Anglican Priests claim the right to hear *confessions* and pronounce *absolution*. Against these claims we may set the teaching of the New Testament:

(*a*) There is one Mediator, and only one, between God and men, Christ Jesus (1 Tim. ii. 5).

(*b*) Jesus Christ is the High Priest (Heb. iii. 1); and every believer is a priest with the right to draw near to

God and to offer sacrifices of praise and thanksgiving
(1 Peter ii. 5, 9 and Rev. i. 6).

(4) *Apostolical Succession.* The High Anglicans and
Romanists claim that Ordination is valid only when performed by a Bishop, and by a Bishop who derives his own
Orders by unbroken *succession from the Apostles.* Hence
the Roman Church denies the validity of Anglican Orders,
and both Churches deny the validity of the Nonconformist
Ministry.

The general reply of Nonconformists is to point out that
the true Apostolical Succession is one of faith and of
character. In Gal. iii. 6-9 St. Paul emphasizes the fact
that the true children of Abraham, who have a claim to
the blessings promised to him, are not his descendants
according to the flesh, but those who are his followers in
faith and character. Similarly the true Apostolical Succession is not a matter of any external ceremony, but the continuation of the faith, devotion, and zeal of the Apostles.

4. *The Roman Catholic Claim.* The Roman Church
claims to stand in a unique position as the one true Church,
possessing the only true Ministry ; and it argues that :
(*a*) St. Peter was the founder of the Church of Rome, and
its first Bishop. (*b*) Christ constituted him the foundation
of the Church, and gave to him " the power of the keys,"
by which Romanists understand the right to admit to
Heaven (see Matt. xvi. 15-19).

To this Protestants reply as follows:

(1) There is no evidence that St. Peter founded the
Church of Rome, or was its first Bishop. It is not absolutely certain that he even visited Rome.

(2) There is no evidence of an unbroken succession of
ordinations by Bishops from the earliest Bishops of Rome
to the present day.

(3) Some of the Popes, or Bishops of Rome, were unbelievers, of grossly immoral life ; and it is inconceivable
that any spiritual grace could flow through such a channel.

(4) The Romanist interpretation of Matt. xvi. 18, 19, is
entirely wrong. For:

(*a*) The " Rock " of which Christ spoke as the foundation of His Church was not the person of Peter, but His own Divine Person, in which Peter had just confessed his belief. He gave to Simon personally the name of Peter, i.e., " a rock," because he was the first to make the confession.

It is very suggestive that Jesus uses two different words for "rock" in this passage. Some are a little afraid to press the distinction, but we almost certainly have the right to do so. Jesus says that the foundation of the Church is the *petra,* which means a solid mass of natural *bed-rock,* whilst Peter is described as a *petros,* that is, *a* rock or *piece* of rock suitable for building into the fabric. Thus the confessed Christ is the *petra,* or *the* rock ; and every confessing Christian, beginning with Peter, is a *petros,* or *a* rock built into the fabric.

This is confirmed by the teaching of St. Peter himself, who in 1 Peter ii. 4-6 speaks of Christ as the " chief corner-stone," and of believers generally as " living stones." In 1 Cor. iii. 11, St. Paul insists that Christ is the one and only Foundation ; though according to Eph. ii. 20, " the apostles and prophets " (not Peter only) are a secondary foundation, since they were the first to believe, and so formed the first course of stones built into the fabric.

(*b*) The promise to give to Peter the " keys " has been ingeniously interpreted as meaning that it was to be his privilege to declare the Kingdom open, as some honoured visitor receives a key and declares the building open in the case of a new Church. If this be the right meaning, the promise was certainly fulfilled to him at Pentecost.

(*c*) The authority to " bind " and to " loose " is described in Matt. xvi. 19 as given to St. Peter. But in Matt. xviii. 18 we read that precisely the same authority was given to the whole body of disciples. The nature of this authority was explained on p. 133.

That the Roman Catholic claim for St. Peter is mistaken is clear from the facts: (1) that, within a few moments of the great promise, the Saviour sternly rebuked him as

" Satan " ; (2) that, whilst St. Peter unquestionably held a conspicuous and honoured place in the Apostolic Church, neither he nor any one else at that time seems to have imagined that his position was in any way unique.

CHAPTER XI

THE SACRAMENTS

OUR Lord was so far tender towards our human craving for things visible, that, in establishing the most inward and spiritual of religions, He ordained two visible ceremonies, Baptism and the Lord's Supper.

These are known as the *Sacraments,* the name being derived from a Latin word which meant: (1) the sum deposited as a *pledge* of good faith in making a bargain, and (2) the soldier's *oath of allegiance* to the Emperor. Both these ideas enter into our public sacramental services, for each of them involves a pledge made before others and a vow of dedication to God. Yet these belong to the human side of the Sacraments, for they represent what we do for God ; and the name Sacraments is defective, since it gives no hint of the greater things which God does for us through them. All Christian Churches observe them except the Quakers (or Friends) and the Salvation Army.

The following is a simple definition: " A Sacrament is a rite ordained by Christ Himself, to be a sign and a means of spiritual grace."

The essentials of a Sacrament are, therefore:

(1) Appointment by Christ Himself for all His followers.

(2) Some material symbol of spiritual things.

The Roman Church recognizes seven Sacraments, the five additional ones being Confirmation, Penance, Matrimony, Ordination, and Extreme Unction, commonly called the Last Sacrament. These ceremonies can only be performed by the clergy, whose power is therefore greater than in any other Church. Penance imposed by a priest after Confession, and Extreme Unction, administered as necessary for salvation, are both unscriptural. Marriage and Ordination are rightly accompanied by religious ceremonies ; but these are not Sacraments, for Christian people are under no obligation to marry or to take Orders. Confirmation is often a very helpful service ; but it was not ordained by Christ, and is, therefore, not a Sacrament. Indeed, its Scripture warrant is most trifling: the statement that St. Paul and others confirmed the Churches which had been founded on the previous journey (Acts xv. 32, 41) suggests merely that they encouraged them. Many Protestants very rightly value a service for the recognition of young Christians ; but even those who call it Confirmation, like the Anglicans and the Lutherans, do not call it a Sacrament.

A.—CHRISTIAN BAPTISM

A common type of definition is as follows: " Baptism by water into the Name of the Father and of the Son and of the Holy Spirit, is the rite of admission into the visible Church." So far all the Churches agree, though the Roman and Anglican Churches go further.

It should be noted that we baptize *into* the Name, not *in* the Name, of God. We do not perform the ceremony on God's behalf, as an official of State acts in the King's name. God's *Name* stands for all that He is, so that in baptizing into the Name of God we baptize *into God,* i.e., into His love, mercy, and power, claiming all these on behalf of the one baptized.

We use the three-fold Name because that is the Christian title for God, and Baptism is a specifically Christian ceremony. Jews and Mohammedans might speak of " God," but only Christians can speak of " the Father, the Son, and the Holy Ghost."

There are three great questions in dispute in connexion with the subject of Baptism.

1. *The Purpose and Results of Baptism.* The statement of John the Baptist, " I indeed baptize you with water . . . He shall baptize you with the Holy Ghost " (Matt. iii. 11), suggests that there are *two kinds of Baptism* referred to in the New Testament: (1) *Water Baptism*

which is man's or the Church's Baptism ; and (2) *Holy Ghost Baptism,* which is Christ's Baptism. The fact that Jesus did not baptize, though His disciples did so (John iv. 2), confirms us in making this distinction ; and the fact that the Twelve apparently received no Baptism by water except that of John, suggests that the Baptism of the Holy Ghost is the distinctively *Christian* Baptism on which our Saviour laid stress. If we are at liberty to carry this distinction through our whole study of the subject, many of the difficulties will disappear, and it will be seen that there is truth on both sides in some of the controversies that have arisen.

Baptism by water is *the ceremony of admission to the Church on earth,* and corresponds to similar ceremonies by which new members are recognized in many societies and guilds. Like most such ceremonies, the Baptismal Service includes a vow or pledge, more or less explicitly stated. In the case of adults, the vow is, of course, taken by the candidate himself. In the case of infants, a promise is made on the child's behalf in the Anglican Church ; whilst in Nonconformist Churches the service is rather a promise made by the parents to dedicate their child to God and train him aright.

The results of Baptism. The Roman Catholics, and, at any rate, the stricter Anglicans, go a great deal further, and contend that Baptism (1) regenerates, (2) admits into the family of God, (3) is necessary to salvation.

All this is obviously true of that Baptism of the Spirit which Christ gives at Conversion ; for that does regenerate and make us children of God, and is necessary to salvation ; whilst the witness of the Spirit granted at the same time is certainly a sign to us that we are admitted into the spiritual Church or the family of God.

But Nonconformists maintain that such results cannot be claimed for the Church's Baptism by water, and that this ceremony can, in the nature of things, do no more than admit us to the earthly company of Christ's followers.

The *objections to the doctrine of Baptismal Regeneration* are as follows:

(1) The whole spirit of the Gospel is against the idea

that salvation depends upon any external ceremony. The doctrine of regeneration by human Baptism is very similar to that great error which St. Paul denounced so vehemently in the Epistle to the Galatians, namely, the belief that salvation was by faith *plus* circumcision, and not by faith alone.

(2) The adults of whom we are told in the New Testament were all baptized after conversion, that is, they were not baptized to make them Christians, but because, having believed in Christ, they wished to be recognized as His followers. Similarly, no Church baptizes adults to-day, either at home or on the mission field, without a confession of the Christian Faith and evidences of consistent life.

(3) As regards infants, the statement of F. W. Robertson that " Baptism makes a child of God in the same sense in which coronation makes a king," exactly represents the Nonconformist position. For coronation does not *make* a king, it is only a public acknowledgment that he *is* king, and a king is not generally crowned until at least a year after his accession. Human Baptism does not make a child of God ; but recognizes one who is a child of God ; and the justification for Infant Baptism is that in their innocency they are dear to God and are already members of His family.

(4) The Scripture support is most unsubstantial. The words: " Except a man be born of water and of the Spirit " (John iii. 5), do not refer to Baptism with water, but to that *cleansing* of the nature which is an essential part of the New Birth. Similarly the words: " The washing of regeneration and renewing of the Holy Ghost " (Titus iii. 5) do not refer to human Baptism, but to the *purifying* of the nature which takes place in Regeneration. It would be as reasonable to see a reference to human Baptism in the words, " And I will sprinkle clean water upon you, and ye shall be clean " (Ezek. xxxvi. 25). There is no mention of the ceremony of Baptism in connexion with any of these passages, though each of them describes a purification of the heart which forms part of the spiritual Baptism which Christ bestows.

(5) The logical consequences of the doctrine are monstrous and incredible ; for, if it be true, all who die unbaptized, even infants and the heathen, are lost. Under the influence of this belief Baptism has sometimes been reduced to a grotesque and blasphemous mockery, the heathen being baptized by Roman Catholic priests, in former days, in vast crowds, without the slightest conception of the meaning of the Christian Faith. The average High Churchman to-day escapes this monstrous conclusion by consigning those who die unbaptized to "the *uncovenanted* mercies of God," i.e., mercies which may be vouchsafed, but which are not promised.

The question remains, Is it *binding* upon Christian people to be baptized? The Nonconformist reply is that the spiritual Baptism is obviously essential ; and that the Church's Baptism cannot be lightly ignored, seeing that the Master Himself was baptized by John and ordained the rite for His Church. The unbaptized Christian is guilty of neglecting an injunction of Christ, and also suffers if he fails to identify himself with the avowed followers of Christ. In the case of infants, their parents are guilty of neglecting an ordinance instituted by Christ, and deprive their children of real privileges by not claiming for them their place among the people of God on earth.

2. *Infant Baptism.* All Churches, except the Baptist, maintain that infants are fit subjects for human Baptism. Yet in some ways the Baptist position seems both reasonable and attractive:

(1) It is obvious that the Baptism of the Spirit cannot be consciously experienced in infancy.

(2) The baptisms of which we find detailed record in the Acts were those of adults.

(3) If Baptism involves a personal confession of faith and a personal oath of allegiance to Christ, it cannot be administered before years of discretion are reached.

(4) Some service which affords young people the opportunity of making a public profession of Christ is a very great practical gain to the Church ; and most Churches which practise Infant Baptism find it necessary to add to

Baptism either Confirmation or some corresponding service for the recognition of new members..

(5) It need hardly be said that where converts, either on the mission field or at home, have not been baptized in infancy, *all* Churches practise Adult Baptism.

Yet if the essence of Baptism is the claim to share in the blessings of the New Covenant, and to have a place among the people of God on earth, there are good reasons for administering it in *infancy :*

(1) Baptism, as the outward token of admission to the New Covenant, corresponds to Circumcision, the outward token of admission to the Old Covenant; and children were circumcised when only eight days old.

(2) If, as our Saviour said, " of such is the Kingdom of Heaven," children are pre-eminently fit to be publicly acknowledged as belonging to Christ and to His Church.

(3) It is incredible that there were no young children in the households which are described as having been baptized as complete households (Acts xvi. 15, 33 ; 1 Cor. i. 16).

(4) Those who baptize in infancy recognize that the place in the Church of Christ, which is claimed for the child by his parents, must be claimed afresh by the child himself when he reaches years of discretion. Yet the claim is not unreal. In some countries the infant son of the reigning sovereign has been recognized as a Colonel in the army from the day of his birth. The rank has been so far real that his name has appeared in the Army List, and his regiment has acknowledged him as its chief. But, if his position is to remain real when he grows older, he will have to adopt as his own his father's purpose that he should be a soldier.

3. *Sprinkling or Immersion ?* The Baptist Churches differ from others in insisting further that Baptism must be by *immersion* or *dipping*. They argue that:

(1) The word " baptize " strictly means to dip.

(2) The New Testament narrative seems to indicate dipping in running water.

The other Churches do not dispute that immersion was a common mode of Baptism ; and an Anglican or Methodist minister is perfectly free, and willing, to immerse those who have conscientious scruples on the matter. But they deny that immersion is the only legitimate mode of Baptism.

(1) It is by no means certain that the word from which " baptize " is derived always means to dip. The disciples were " baptized " with the Holy Ghost at Pentecost ; but they were certainly not immersed in Him. St. Paul, in 1 Cor. x. 2, speaks of the children of Israel as being " baptized unto Moses " at the crossing of the Red Sea. But they were not immersed, for they went over dry-shod ; and, if they were " baptized," it can only have been by the sprinkling of the spray.

(2) The New Testament narratives do not all point to immersion. For instance, there can have been no stream of water available for the Baptism of the Philippian Jailor, which took place in prison. Even where there was running water, it seems probable that the rite was administered by *pouring* whilst the parties stood in shallow water. This is confirmed by the fact that the blessing of Pentecost is described as being " poured forth " by Christ (Acts ii. 33).

(3) No detail of mode can be essential to a Christian ceremony, and the Baptist insistence on this point is strangely out of keeping with their general attitude towards matters of ritual. Logically, they ought also to insist on an exact reproduction of the Lord's Supper, and observe it as a complete meal, taken reclining. The reasonable view is, surely, that just as the morsel of bread and the sip of wine suffice as symbols in the one case, so the few drops of water suffice as the symbol in the other.

B.—THE LORD'S SUPPER

Definition. This service is also known as *the Sacrifice of the Mass* in Roman Catholic and some Anglican Churches, as the *Eucharist* (or Thanksgiving) in many Anglican Churches, and as the *Holy Communion* among Low Churchmen and Nonconformists.

The following definition would be very generally accepted: " The Lord's Supper is the use of bread and wine as our Lord Himself commanded, signifying the New Covenant in His Blood, and the spiritual nourishment which by faith we receive from Him ; it is also a pledge of our devotion to Him, and of our union with one another."

The form of the ceremony varies greatly, ranging from the simple " breaking of bread " amongst the Plymouth Brethren to the stately ritual of the Roman Mass.

1. *Its Purpose and Value.* Following the definition given above, the purpose of this Sacrament may be stated thus:

(1) It is an act of *Obedience* to an injunction of our Lord given under particularly solemn circumstances.

(2) It is an act of *Remembrance,* in which we call to remembrance—(i) our Lord Himself ; (ii) His dying Love ; (iii) the New Covenant to which His Death admits us.

(3) It is an Act of *Appropriation,* in which we claim as our own the merits of His Death and the blessings of the Covenant.

(4) It is an act of *Spiritual Nourishment,* in which we feed upon Christ under the symbols of bread and wine. The essence of the Christian life is such a personal union with Christ that He dwells within us. This union may be claimed and realized by prayer and in other ways. But, in the experience of many, the most direct and vivid way of realizing it is to partake of the sacred symbols, believing that as we do so in faith Christ enters into our life and infuses into us His strength. We know that a material wave of air striking the ear reappears in the mind in a non-material form as a musical sound. The Sacred Bread is bread, and remains bread ; but it has a spiritual counterpart of which it is the symbol, and, when it is eaten in faith, that spiritual counterpart is realized as the presence of Christ in the heart. The sacramental Elements are not, in themselves, food for the soul ; but they are tokens

of spiritual food endorsed by Christ Himself and, when they are used as such in faith, the soul actually receives the food of which they are the promise.

(5) To partake of the Lord's Supper involves a *Confession* of faith in Christ: the service is public, and, therefore, the mere fact of a man's presence as a communicant amounts to a public avowal of faith in Christ and loyalty to Him.

(6) It is an act of *Personal Consecration*. Almost inevitably the service includes a definite re-dedication of ourselves to Christ ; and, inasmuch as the service is public, it becomes a public " pledge of our devotion to Him."

(7) It is an act of *Fellowship* or *Communion* with other believers. The service reminds us very forcibly of our connexion with our fellow-Christians, not only in our own Church but everywhere, seeing that almost all Christian societies observe this ordinance in some form or other. In all ages the common meal has been the token of friendship and of union: friendship is fostered by hospitality and in many societies the annual re-union by which the spirit of comradeship is maintained takes the form of a dinner. It was thus almost inevitable that the common meal should become the " token of our union with one another." This aspect of the Sacrament is seen in the collection usually made on behalf of the poor members of the Church ; and, where a liturgy is used, it also appears in the prayer " for the whole estate of Christ's Church militant here upon earth."

· 2. " *The Real Presence.*" *Various Views.* Whilst almost all would agree with most of what has been stated above as to the use and value of the Lord's Supper, there are very great differences of opinion as to what actually takes place in the administration of this Sacrament. This is indicated by the various senses in which the words, " the *Real Presence of Christ,*" are understood in different Churches.

(1) Very extreme Protestants regard the service as a memorial ceremony and no more. The Elements are

reminders of Christ, but have no spiritual significance. Christ is present to bless His people, but only in the same sense in which He is present in any other meeting for worship.

(2) Most Protestant Churches, e.g., the Methodist and Presbyterian, agree that Christ is not present in the Elements, and that they remain unchanged. Yet they are sacred *symbols*, representing the unseen Christ ; and those who partake of them in faith, but they only, actually experience in their hearts the real presence of Christ, of whom the Bread and the Wine are the symbols.

(3) The Lutheran Church holds that there is an actual change in the Elements called *Consubstantiation*, as the result of which Christ's Body is present " along with " the Bread, which is now bread and something more. On this view, even those who partake without faith receive the Body of Christ, though they do so unworthily and to their condemnation.

(4) The Roman Church maintains that there is a complete change in the Elements called *Transubstantiation*, by which they cease to be bread and wine, though they retain the appearance of bread and wine, and become literally the Body, Blood, Soul, and Divinity of Christ. One natural consequence of this view is the Adoration of the Host, or worship of the consecrated wafer. Another inevitable result is that the position of the Priest who is able to work this miracle is enormously enhanced.

It need hardly be said that this doctrine finds no support in Scripture ; for, if, as the Romanists contend, we are bound to interpret literally Christ's statement that the Bread is His Body, we ought also to treat literally His statements that He is the Door and the Vine. It is clear that the one phrase is as purely figurative as the others.

F

CHAPTER XII

The Solemn Events of the Future

WE come now to the consideration of those great and solemn events of the future which are commonly described as *The Last Things*. We enter a region of deep mystery, and can only speak on any of these subjects with great caution and reserve, for in the nature of things our knowledge of them must be very limited. What we do know is derived from prophecies, many of which are expressed in highly figurative language, whilst some of them appear to be inconsistent with others. Prophecy is always difficult of interpretation beforehand: the predictions of the Old Testament were amply fulfilled in Christ, yet devout Jews in His day had derived from their study of those very Scriptures a completely different conception of what the Messiah was to be. The prophecies of the New Testament will, no doubt, receive their fulfilment in due course ; but that fulfilment will almost certainly bring many surprises to us all. For the present the details of their meaning are largely hidden from us ; and, meanwhile, their purpose is rather to create in us a spirit of solemn expectation than to lighten our darkness.

A.—THE END OF THE WORLD

Science agrees with the Bible that this World, which originated in Time, cannot possibly endure for ever as the home of life. In the natural course of things, a time will come when it will be too cold to sustain life any longer. After that, if not before, the end may come, either by a collision with some other heavenly body, resulting in a stupendous conflagration ; or by a gradual loss of speed in the Earth's rotation round the Sun, until the point is reached at which it can no longer resist the attraction of the Sun, when it will fall into it and be consumed.

Similarly, Science foresees an end to the Universe as a whole.

The Bible connects the End of the World more distinctly with a direct act of God ; but it, too, speaks of a great conflagration (2 Peter ii. 10), which may be brought about in one of the ways just named.

B.—THE SECOND COMING OF CHRIST

Closely connected with the End of the World in the New Testament is the Second Coming of Christ, often called the *Parousia,* from a Greek word which means " coming " or " presence." The subject was very prominent in the teaching of Jesus, especially towards the close of His ministry (see Matt. xxiv. and xxv. and parallels in Mark and Luke, and John xiv. 3). From the Epistles we find that it was the continual hope and inspiration of the disciples, so much so that the words " The Lord is at hand," most probably in the sense, " His Coming is near," formed a kind of password by which Christians recognized one another (Phil. iv. 6). It occurs in the Aramaic form *Maranatha* in 1 Cor. xvi. 22.

1. *Early expectation.* There are many signs that the Apostolic Church anticipated this triumphant Return of their Lord as almost immediate. In the Thessalonian Church some looked for it so soon that they abandoned their daily occupations, under the impression that it was not worth while to concern themselves with earthly things which were so soon to pass away. St. Paul's chief object in writing his two letters to this Church was to correct these misapprehensions, and rebuke those who were bringing reproach upon the Church through their thriftlessness and idleness.

Yet St. Paul himself in the earlier part of his ministry unquestionably expected that he would live to see his Lord's Return. Cf. " Then *we* that are alive, that are left, shall, together with them, be caught up in the clouds to meet the Lord in the air " (1 Thess. iv. 17) ; and " For the trumpet shall sound, and the dead shall be raised incorruptible, and *we* shall be changed " (1 Cor. xv. 52). We can trace in 2 Cor. i. 8, 9 the change that comes over his views as the result of a serious illness which befell him in the interval between the writing of the two letters. He finds now that he must trust " in God which raiseth the dead," and must expect to be amongst those who have to be raised from the dead when Christ comes.

The rumour that John " should not die " (John xxi. 23) was only possible in a community that believed the End to be very near ; and the vivid expectation is especially prominent in James v. 8.

2. *The teaching of Jesus.* The disciples derived their ideas of the Future from the teaching of Jesus, and this mistaken expectation of His speedy Coming can only have arisen from the meaning they attached to some of His words. There are certainly some sayings of His which might naturally be interpreted in this sense ; and there are even some writers who assert that Jesus Himself was mistaken, and Himself expected an early Return. This is a very serious error to impute to Him. The evidence adduced consists of such passages as, " This generation shall not pass away, till all these things be accomplished " (Matt. xxiv. 34).

The truth appears to be that the teaching of Jesus on the subject refers, not only to His final Coming, but to many manifestations of His presence, power and glory, that were to occur before the End, some of them very soon, such as the Transfiguration, Pentecost, and the Destruction of Jerusalem. Such events as these were adequate fulfilments of His predictions concerning that generation ; and we may see in many striking manifestations of His power since then what may be described as comings of the Lord, for, in a certain sense, He is always coming: cf. " Lo, I am with you alway " (Matt. xxviii. 20).

3. *Main conclusions.* Confining ourselves to those sayings of Jesus and His Apostles which distinctly refer to the Second Coming proper, there are a few broad facts which stand out in the teaching of the New Testament on this subject:

(1) The Second Coming is described as a visible return to earth (Matt. xxvi. 64 ; Acts i. 11).

(2) It will be glorious and majestic, the coming of a King, in marked contrast with the humiliation of His First Advent (Matt. xvi. 27, xxv. 31).

(3) It will be sudden and unexpected (Matt. xxiv. 42-44; Luke xvii. 26—30).

(4) The time is quite unknown (Matt. xxiv. 36).

(5) It will be preceded by a terrible outbreak of sin and apostasy, which St. Paul describes as the revelation, or *parousia,* of " the man of sin " (2 Thess. ii. 1—10).

(6) It will be the complete and final triumph of righteousness (2 Thess. ii. 8).

The Millennarian View

A single passage, Rev. xx. 1-10, has led some in all ages of the Christian Church to another view of the Second Coming, which differs greatly from the above. According to this there will be a preliminary visible Return, followed by a physical resurrection of the saints or, at least, of the martyrs (the *First* Resurrection); they will then reign with Christ for a *millennium* (i.e., 1,000 years), during which time Satan will be " bound "; there will then be a great apostasy and a general outbreak of evil, leading up to the final conflict between Sin and Righteousness; and this will be followed by *another* visible Return of Christ to raise *all* the dead (the *Second* Resurrection), and to judge the world.

Those who hold this view do so with great tenacity, and anticipate its fulfilment with almost daily expectation. They are called *Pre-millennarians,* because they expect the Return of Christ to be *before* the Millennium, the prefix *pre-* meaning before; or sometimes simply *Millennarians,* because they give such prominence to the Millennium.

The *objections* to this view are so weighty that it has never been accepted except by a small minority.

(1) Its only direct support is found in a solitary passage in the most obscure book of the Bible; and this is insufficient foundation for a doctrine of such importance.

(2) The great mass of Scripture teaching is against it.

and it directly conflicts with St. Paul's statement that there will be no Return until *after* the great apostasy (2 Thess. ii. 3).

(3) The scheme of events is unnatural and fantastic, and would be exceedingly difficult to accept even if it were the teaching of Scripture generally ; for it implies *two* Returns, *two* Resurrections, and an apparently purposeless interval of a thousand years.

(4) The whole conception, as generally understood by its advocates, is material: the saints are to be gathered to Christ with *physical* bodies, and to reign for a thousand years, presumably in some material place.

But if we reject the Pre-millennarian view, we have still to find a satisfactory interpretation for Rev. xx. 1-10. In a book so full of symbolism as the Revelation we have the right to regard much of the language as figurative. If we consent to read the passage in this way, it appears that:

(1) The Millennium is the present history of the Christian Church, which began with the First Advent of Christ, and is in progress now: it is the dispensation of the Gospel. The thousand years represent a very long period, the age during which the Church on earth will last.

(2) The "binding of Satan" means that since the Advent of Christ his power has been partially restrained, for Sin received a mortal defeat upon the Cross. "There is one that restraineth *now*" (2 Thess. ii. 7) probably refers to the Roman Empire and other systems of government, which have acted or now act as a check upon lawlessness and sin.

(3) The First Resurrection and the Reign of the Saints may be interpreted in two ways.

(*a*) St. Paul describes conversion as a spiritual resurrection, by which the believer is raised from the death of sin to the life of righteousness (see Rom. vi. 4, 5) ; and he also speaks of sitting with Christ in the heavenly places as the present privilege of all believers (see Eph. ii. 5, 6).

It cannot be these experiences, however, which are referred to in the Revelation, for they belong to the present life, whilst the Revelation speaks of experiences that follow death, and particularly mentions the martyrs (xx. 4).

(b) A much more satisfactory interpretation is that those who are cut off from the warfare of Christ's Church on earth, some of them by martyrdom, are not really cut off from His warfare and victory. In their spirits they are restored to activity, though we cannot see them (the First Resurrection), and they share with their Lord in that Sovereignty which He is winning by the triumphs of the Gospel.

(4) On either view the loosing of Satan (Rev. xx. 7) corresponds to that revelation of " the man of sin " or " the lawless one " and that general apostasy, of which St. Paul speaks, as immediately preceding the Return of Christ (2 Thess. ii. 3 and 8).

The deeper significance of the doctrine of the Second Advent is that, in the end of things, right will gain a final and endless victory ; and that the decay of the Universe will not mean a return to nothingness, but will be the manifestation of the spiritual and eternal reality, of which the visible Universe is but the passing shadow.

C.—THE RESURRECTION OF THE DEAD

The New Testament teaches that the Second Coming is to be followed immediately by the Resurrection of the Dead (see John v. 25-29 ; 1 Cor. xv. 52 ; 1 Thess. iv. 16). This is a feature of the life to come which has no parallel in other religions.

Two passages in the Old Testament (Job xix. 25-27 and Psa. xvi. 10, 11), appear to teach the doctrine, and the latter of them is quoted by St. Peter, in Acts ii. 25-28, as a prophecy of the Resurrection of Christ. But the references in the Old Testament are so few that some commentators contend that, even in the case of these two passages, the doctrine is read into them by the Christian reader, and that, in their context, they merely represent the speakers' vivid hope of restoration to life and health after being brought near to the grave by sickness. However that may be, the doctrine was not a matter of common knowledge or belief in Old Testament times.

But, as was stated on p. 104, the Jewish belief in
immortality became much more definite in the interval
between the two Testaments ; and in our Saviour's day,
except among the Sadducees, there was also a widespread
belief in the Resurrection of the Body.

The Intermediate State

It is very important that we should understand the
teaching of the Bible with reference to the present condition
of the departed, or what is called in Christian doctrine the
Intermediate State. For this purpose certain Bible words
should be carefully noted.

In the Old Testament the word *Sheol* is used for the
underworld, or place of the dead. It does not mean the
place of torment, and it is very unfortunate that the A.V.
has so often translated it *hell*. It is a purely neutral word,
and, if it is to be translated, it is best to use the word
grave. The R.V., however, does not generally attempt to
translate it, but renders it *Sheol* (see Ps. xviii. 5 ; cxxxix. 8;
but note Ps. lv. 15 and Jonah ii. 2).

In the New Testament we find two words:

(1) *Hades*, which exactly corresponds to *Sheol*, and is
the abode of the dead, good and bad alike. Here again
the A.V. often makes the mistake of rendering it *hell ;*
but the R.V. always leaves it in the form *Hades*. Cf. the
two versions in Acts ii. 27 and Rev. xx. 13. Similarly, the
clause, " He descended into Hell," in the Apostles' Creed
should be, " He descended into Hades (or the grave)."

(2) *Gehenna*, which occurs less frequently, comes from
Ge-Hinnom, or the Valley of Hinnom, the name of the
spot where the rubbish of the city of Jerusalem was
deposited, and where fires were continually burning for
the destruction of the refuse. It became the common
name among the Jews for the place of torment, and may
properly be translated *hell* (Matt. x. 28 and xxiii. 15, in
the R.V., and note the margin).

The frequent use of such neutral and colourless words
as *Sheol* and *Hades*, and our Saviour's description of
death as a *sleep*, might seem to indicate that the present

condition of the dead is a dim and shadowy, half-conscious existence, which can hardly be called life.

But the parable of the Rich man and Lazarus (Luke xvi. 19-31), which speaks of the rich man as being in Hades, not in Gehenna, indicates that, even in this Intermediate State, a change of condition takes place: there is the "great gulf fixed," and a measure of conscious bliss for the good and of torment for the wicked. This accords with the interpretation of the "First Resurrection" suggested on p. 161, according to which the martyr souls quickly pass from the sleep, which is the immediate result of death, into renewed spiritual activity; though that new life is not really complete without the Resurrection Body.

Thus there seem to be three stages indicated : (1) The sleep ; (2) the awaking to spiritual activity in the "First Resurrection"; (3) the restoration to full and perfect life by the Resurrection of the Body, in the case of the righteous ; and three corresponding stages in the case of the wicked.

Have we the right to say of the sainted dead that they are in *Heaven*? It is safer not to do so, for it appears that the perfect bliss of Heaven and the real torment of Hell do not begin until after the Resurrection and the Judgment. But the New Testament does permit us to say concerning the dead in Christ that they are "blessed" and that they "rest" (Rev. xiv. 13), that they are "with Christ" (Phil. i. 23), and that they are "in Paradise" (Luke xxiii. 43), though Paradise is not identical with Heaven. Paradise may perhaps be described as the purely spiritual world, Heaven as far as Heaven exists at present ; but it will only become Heaven in the full and complete sense by the addition of the transfigured and glorified Universe.

The Resurrection Body

The doctrine of the Resurrection is necessary because the Bible regards the body as an essential part of the man, so that a disembodied spirit is only capable of a somewhat shadowy and incomplete existence. If the soul is to enjoy a full life in the Future, it must receive some kind of body to serve as its tenement and its instrument, and to enable it to communicate with other souls.

The new body. The Resurrection is represented as following immediately on the Second Coming (1 Thess. iv. 16). The great passage on the subject is 1 Cor. xv. 20-57, and in it several points are emphasized:

(1) It will *not* be *the same* body. The earthly body is material, and in due course decays, changes into other substances, and may even enter into the grass growing upon the grave, and so pass into the bodies of animals that feed upon the grass.

(2) It is a *spiritual* body (*v.* 44), for Heaven is a spiritual world. A body is the tenement and instrument appropriate to the soul in the world in which it has to live. In this material world we require material bodies, but the Resurrection body will be some envelope for the soul that will serve its purposes in a spiritual world. Some have conceived it as a body of that mysterious substance, ether.

(3) It will be very *different* from the present body (*vv.* 36-38), perhaps as different as the growing plant is from the seed sown ; for the seed and the growing plant are both bodies for the same little bit of plant life.

(4) It will be a *glorious* body (*v.* 43), perhaps differing as much in beauty from the present body as the butterfly differs from the grub.

(5) It will be *connected* in some way with the present body, just as the beautiful plant is connected with the seed. The process is not described as the creation of a completely new body, it is the glorification of the present body.

The nearest approach to a description of this body is found in the statement that it will resemble *the body of Christ's glory,* that is, the body which He has in His glorified life (Phil. iii. 21). It may help us if we consider the nature of the body of Christ after His Resurrection.

(1) It completely took the place of the body laid in the grave, for the grave was empty.

(2) It bore some resemblance to the former body, for His disciples were able to recognize Him. Yet some change had taken place, for they did not recognize Him easily: e.g., Mary took Him for the gardener, and the two on the way to Emmaus did not know Him.

(3) It was not a purely material body. He partook of food, and pointed out to Thomas that He had flesh and bones. Yet He appears to have been able to move instantaneously from place to place, and to enter the upper room without unfastening the door. At this stage it seems to have been a semi-material body, for it had some material and some " ethereal " characteristics.

(4) At the Ascension it shed the last traces of the material, and became a " spiritual " body.

In speaking of the " glory " of Christ's body, St. Paul may also have had in mind the dazzling whiteness which enveloped Him at the Transfiguration.

Two far-reaching truths are implied in the doctrine of the Resurrection of the Body:

1. Salvation is not merely salvation of the soul, but the salvation of the man in his whole being, body, soul and spirit.

2. Rom. viii. 20-23 suggests that the whole Creation and the material Universe will in perishing undergo some similar transformation, and be represented in the Future by some glorified and spiritual counterpart. If this be so, the " new heaven " and the " new earth " of Rev. xxi. 1 will arise out of the ashes of the old in a spiritual and imperishable form, and nothing will " be cast as rubbish to the void."

D.—THE UNIVERSAL JUDGMENT

The Bible teaches that the Resurrection of the Dead will be followed by the Judgment of all mankind at the bar of Christ.

The belief in a future Judgment is almost *universal* and *instinctive,* at any rate in all except the most degraded peoples ; for belief in God carries with it the feeling that we are responsible to Him, and shall some day be called to account. In pagan as well as in Christian lands those who love the right have found encouragement in the deep-rooted conviction that virtue must in the end find its reward, and sin its punishment.

The Bible, in both the Old and the New Testaments,

speaks repeatedly of the *Day of the Lord* and the *Day of
Judgment;* and the New Testament places this immediately after the Resurrection of the Dead. Such passages
as Matt. xxv. 31-46 and Rev. xx. 11-15 further describe
the Judgment as taking the form of a *Great Assize,* in
which each man will be judged before the assembled
Universe. The thought is majestic and awe-inspiring, but
it involves some serious difficulties. As we noticed in the
last section, there are some passages of Scripture which
imply that there is a distinction, and a final distinction
("a great gulf fixed"), between the righteous and the
wicked even in the Intermediate State before the Resurrection. This suggests that each man is judged, and his
fate decided, at death, and that the Day of Judgment for
each is the day of his death. This is what we should
naturally expect. We cannot say how far the details of
the scene in the Parable of the Sheep and the Goats are
to be understood literally; and we know so little, that
some incline to leave the form and time of the Judgment
an open question. Yet it is not impossible to harmonize
the two sets of passages; for the destiny of men may be
decided at death, but publicly announced at a great
General Judgment; just as a prisoner who is obviously
guilty of a serious crime is kept in prison, and is not
allowed bail whilst awaiting trial, though his guilt is not
publicly declared until after his formal trial.

There are several points, however, on which the teaching of Scripture leaves us no room for doubt.

1. *The Judgment will be universal.* This implies that :
(*a*) every man will be judged (Rom. xiv. 10-12;
2 Cor. v. 10), and that those who escape detection here
will be discovered there. (*b*) Both good and bad will be
judged. The object of an earthly law-court is to detect
and punish crime; the object of the Judgment will be at
least as much to discover and reward virtue. (*c*) Whether
the Judgment actually takes the form of a Great Assize
or not, it will be a judgment before all the nations, in the
sense that all will come to know the verdict, and henceforth each man will be seen in his true colours, and be
known for what he really is (Luke xii. 2).

2. *The basis of Judgment will be God's Law of Righteousness* (Acts xvii. 31). The law of the State necessarily concerns itself with *crime* and not with *sin ;* e.g., it cannot punish a man for forms of drunkenness or of unchastity that do not directly injure others. The basis of Christ's Judgment will be the law of righteousness, so that it will take account of innumerable sins which are not crimes in human law.

3. *The Judge will be Jesus Christ* (John v. 22 ; Acts x. 42), for He, and He alone, possesses the *qualifications to be the perfect Judge.*

(*a*) *He knows all things.* In human justice the guilty often escape for lack of evidence, and the innocent sometimes suffer through evidence that is false ; but in what are called the Books of God all the facts are recorded, and there can be no error or miscarriage of justice.

(*b*) *He knows the heart.* It is obvious that ideal justice must take account of all the circumstances ; it must be able to measure the force of temptation, and allow for all that handicaps a man in virtue ; and, above all, it must be perfect in its reading of motives. Human justice endeavours, as far as it can, to judge men according to their opportunities ; and sentences passed on similar offences often vary greatly in their severity on this account. Yet human justice at best knows only a few facts, it does not know the man ; and, therefore, its judgment can never be perfectly just.

(*c*) *He is absolutely just.* All good judges do their utmost to act strictly impartially. But many things may serve to inspire a certain prejudice for or against a prisoner, quite against the judge's will. Christ's knowledge of the hearts of men is so complete and direct that He necessarily judges men as they really are, not as they appear to be.

(*d*) *He is perfectly sympathetic.* He knows our human weakness, and He alone can make perfect allowances for our difficulties. He is God, and therefore it is true of Him that " He knoweth our frame, He remembereth that we are dust " (Psa. ciii. 14).

The Judgment of Christians. It appears from such passages as John xii. 48 that, in the case of those who have known the Christian Gospel, men are to be judged chiefly by their *attitude towards Christ,* according as they repent and accept Him, or not. Rom. ii. 6 and 2 Cor. v. 10, represent the Judgment as a detailed survey of " the deeds done in the body," but it is not to be supposed that these will be reckoned like points in an examination: their chief importance will consist in the light that they throw on the attitude of the man's heart towards Christ.

The Judgment of the heathen. It is obvious that those who have never heard of Christ cannot be judged on this principle. St. Paul treats the case of the *heathen* in Rom. ii. 12-16, and states that they will be judged according to *such light and knowledge as they have,* for none are altogether without knowledge of God and of right. Further, it is almost indisputable that in the parable of the Sheep and the Goats (Matt. xxv. 31-46) our Saviour is dealing only with the case of the heathen. The reasons for this supposition are that: (i) any Jewish hearer would understand the words " the nations " to mean the *heathen,* for they were accustomed to speak of all who were not Jews as " the nations," so much so that the A.V. often renders the word " heathen," cf. the A.V. and R.V. in Psa. ii. 1 and cxxxv. 15. In the New Testament the words are generally rendered " the heathen " in the A.V. and " the Gentiles " in the R.V., cf. Matt. vi. 7 and Gal. i. 16 in the two versions. (ii) As we have just seen, Christians are *not* to be judged simply by works of mercy done or left undone, but by their attitude towards Christ. But if we apply this parable to the heathen, we find that the principle of judgment laid down here is very similar to that laid down by St. Paul, the chief difference being that our Lord adds the statement that in their works of mercy the heathen are unconsciously serving the Christ of whom they have not heard.

E.—THE DESTINY OF THE WICKED

In the discussion of this subject we enter a region of dark and dreadful mystery, in which we dare not forget the limitations of our knowledge ; but in which also we dare not forget what we do know as taught both by the Bible and by life itself.

1. *The Inevitable Punishment of Sin*

The instinctive belief. It is a deeply rooted conviction among men that sin brings in its train real and terrible penalties, both now and hereafter. This is confirmed, not only by the teaching of the Bible, but by that of every religion which is sufficiently advanced to have any definite belief concerning the future life. It may seem to be contradicted by the prosperity that often attends the wicked. But even if that prosperity were as complete as it sometimes appears to be, it would only confirm the belief in punishment in the world to come ; for deep down in their hearts men *know* that sin must bring its penalty. There is no instance, however, in which men altogether escape its punishment here: sin always results in moral and spiritual degradation, and " the wages of sin is death " in the sense that it involves the decay and ruin of all that is noblest in our manhood. John Bunyan faces this question in his too little known *Life and Death of Mr. Badman*, in which he sketches the career of a prosperous rogue. He represents him as passing away peacefully, without either penitence or fear, the idea being that his sin has so hardened his heart and conscience that he can no longer believe anything, hope anything, or fear anything in the unseen world. However prosperous the wicked may be, they never escape, even in this life, that degrading and hardening influence.

Punishment inevitable. As regards the Future, our belief in judgment to come may be expressed as a simple and necessary law of life. It is an invariable law of Nature that any moving body must continue to move in the same direction at the same speed for ever, unless some force, such as friction with the air or the ground, comes in to hinder it. In the same way, it is a law of life that men must continue to move in the same direction morally and spiritually in which they are moving now, unless some other influence comes in to hinder them. That is to say, both sin and its consequences naturally and inevitably tend to go on for ever.

Yet there seems to be at present a vague and unreasoned, but very widespread belief that God is a weakly amiable and indulgent Being, who is quite incapable of inflicting pain ; and that there is little or nothing to fear in the Future. Such a belief is quite unaccountable, for it is contradicted by the stern facts of life, by the whole teaching of the Bible, and by every theologian of repute, whatever may be his views as to the form and duration of future punishment. Indeed, there are none who insist more earnestly on the awfulness of the doom of the wicked than some of those who repudiate the older ways of stating the doctrine.

2. The Nature of the Punishment

In spite of our ignorance there are a few general facts of which we may be certain, and which should have made impossible the crude, and even gross, language which has sometimes been used upon this subject.

Non-material. In the case of spirits, punishment must necessarily take a *spiritual* form. All comparisons of Hell to a material fire are, of course, as figurative as the descriptions of the pearly gates and golden streets of Heaven. But anguish of spirit is far more terrible than pain of body ; and more are brought to insanity or suicide through remorse and shame than through physical pain.

Does God torture? There is no need to suppose that the punishment of Sin consists of positive torment directly inflicted by God. Human nature is capable of no worse agony than that which may be produced by (1) the torture of an *evil conscience,* which is " the worm that dieth not "; (2) the sense of *loss,* and the knowledge of what might have been ; (3) the *shame and degradation* of being recognized by others as foul and unclean. To rid our minds of the idea that God positively and directly torments the wicked removes one of the most serious difficulties in our conception of future punishment.

Is Hell a place? In a purely spiritual world, *place* can have comparatively little meaning. Two men sitting side by side may be poles apart in thought, spirit, and feeling : one may be enjoying the ecstasy of the new convert, the other may be suffering the torments of the damned.

> The mind is its own place, and in itself
> Can make a heav'n of hell, a hell of heav'n.

There is thus no need that Heaven and Hell should be regarded as places, in the sense in which we speak of physical places here: the same spiritual world might be Heaven to one and Hell to another ; for each is primarily a spiritual condition. Yet like always tends to gather to like: the slovenly and the vicious prefer to herd together, and, in time, the quarter in which they dwell becomes a slum. So that even if we had not the right to suppose that God makes a rigid separation, it would come about inevitably, and there would eventually be one (or perhaps more) communities of the good, and one (or perhaps more) communities of the evil, dwelling amid conditions suited to them. But Scripture teaches that such a separation will be made by the direct act of God, and immediately (Matt. xiii. 40, xxv. 46).

Gradation. Two or three considerations make it clear that there must be gradations both in punishment and in bliss:

(1) Luke xii. 47, 48 definitely states that the degree of punishment will correspond to the degree of opportunity and responsibility.

(2) Human beings pass into the Future at such different stages of moral development that neither all the good nor all the bad can be on the same footing. It is estimated that at least one-third of the race dies in infancy or very early childhood, before any real moral development or moral choice has become possible. We have the right to assume that they are " saved "; but obviously their moral and spiritual development has yet to begin, and they cannot start in the new life at the same point as a St. John or a St. Paul.

The division. Of those who do not die in early childhood, the great majority appear to be almost neutral in character, neither definitely good nor definitely bad. Is it possible to divide them, men, women, boys and girls, heathen and Christian, trained in good homes and bad, with characters consisting of good and evil mixed in all degrees—is it possible to divide them sharply and finally into two classes? It can be done, but only according to the *tendency* and *direction* of their lives, or according to their *attitude* towards Christ and towards goodness. To use the old illustration, of two little streams flowing close together high up among the mountains and apparently alike, one is flowing East and will find its goal in the Atlantic, the other is flowing West, and will find its goal in the Pacific. Those who are looking towards Christ may be at very different stages in their journey towards Him ; but they are all looking towards Him, and so will continue to move nearer to Him. On the other hand, those whose attitude is towards evil may only just have started, or they may have gone far in their course ; but they will continue to move in the direction they have chosen, towards Sin and away from God. The dividing line is real, " there is a great gulf fixed " (Luke xvi. 26).

Personal choice. It is also clear that a man's destiny is fixed *by his own choice.* In so far as men are " damned," they are not " damned " by God : they damn themselves. Hence the importance of recognizing that it is only the finally impenitent who perish ; and there is relief in the thought that we know little of the secrets of men's hearts, and know little of the mighty influence that the hour of death may bring to bear upon the will. The impressions produced at the supreme moment may suffice to effect a real change of heart almost in an instant. Cases are known of men brought near to death by drowning, who in the critical moment were able to review their whole life, and to whom Christ presented Himself so *vividly* that there was accomplished in that brief space of time a real conversion, which was proved to be genuine by the whole of their after life.

But in the last resort each man goes to " his own place " (Acts i. 25), i.e., the place of his own choice, and the one for which he has fitted himself. Obviously it cannot be otherwise, for without some fundamental change of nature,

will and disposition, an evil man could find no bliss in
Heaven, even if the mercy of God were to bring him
there: Heaven itself would be Hell to him, just as the
atmosphere of a godly home is suffocating to a man of
coarsely sinful life.

3. *The Duration of Future Punishment*

Many, who would perhaps agree with all that has been
said as to the reality and the nature of the punishment of
Sin, are more seriously exercised by the question of its
duration. Is it to last for ever? Is there no hope?
Several theories deserve consideration, namely: (1) Universal Restoration ; (ii) Future Probation ; (iii) Annihilation of the Wicked ; (iv.) Conditional Immortality ;
(v) Eternal Punishment.

(i) *Universal Restoration*

The theory of *Universalism* asserts that after adequate
punishment all are eventually saved, the punishment
serving as a corrective which in the end reforms the sinner.
This theory has some very attractive features:

(1) It satisfies the kindly instincts of our hearts.

(2) It satisfies our sense of justice, and delivers us from
even the suspicion that God is capable of gratuitously
tormenting His creatures for ever.

(3) It appears to accord with two or three passages of
Scripture, e.g., John vi. 37 ; Phil. ii. 10 ; 1 Tim. ii. 4 ;
Eph. i. 10.

(4) It promises a complete and perfect success to the
redeeming work of Christ, whereas the theory of Eternal
Punishment seems to imply that God's purpose may be
partially defeated.

It is a theory that all must wish might be true. But the
objections to it are insuperable:

(1) A great number of passages of Scripture which speak
of the endless duration of punishment are against it, e.g.,
Matt. xviii. 8, xxv. 46 ; Mark ix. 43 ; Luke xvi. 26 ;
2 Thess. i. 9 ; Jude 7 ; Rev. xiv. 11.

(2) The passages quoted in favour of it indicate God's purpose and desire that all should be saved, not that all actually will be saved.

(3) So long as the human will remains the same, it must always be within man's power to resist God ; and whatever gracious or powerful influences God may bring to bear, He will never destroy man's freedom. As Lord Salisbury said of his efforts to prevent Greece from taking up arms against Turkey, a man's friends may do everything to prevent him from committing suicide, except kill him ; and for God to strip men of their free will would be to destroy them as human beings.

(4) Eternal punishment does not imply a vindictive and purposeless infliction of positive torment ; for, as stated above, the punishment may consist in the sense of remorse, of loss, and of ruin.

(5) There will be no such defeat of God's purpose as would imply that He had failed: in the end " every knee shall bow." The sovereignty of King George is acknowledged by loyal citizens in obedient lives, but it is also acknowledged by the most reckless and defiant of criminals in jail, even though they never intend to submit to it. Willingly or unwillingly, every tongue shall confess that Jesus Christ is Lord.

(ii) Future Probation

The theory of *Future Probation* supposes that those who have failed here will be given an opportunity to redeem themselves in the life to come. It is an attractive theory, but the only arguments in its favour are that:

(1) The present life is so short, that it does not seem just that eternal issues should depend upon it, especially as the moral opportunities of some are so small.

(2) One passage, 1 Peter iii. 18-20, is said to state definitely that Christ preached " to the spirits in prison " in the interval between His Death and Resurrection, and to point to further offers of mercy to all the wicked.

Here again the *difficulties* are insuperable.

(a) The present life is not too short, if it is recognized that men are judged according to their opportunities, and that there are gradations of punishment. It is an actual fact of life that there are critical periods upon which a man's whole future career may depend. If a candidate fails to pass into the Civil Service before a given age, he is shut out for life. If the steersman does not alter the course within a given time, his vessel will inevitably become a wreck.

(*b*) Except in the case of very young children, life is not too short to determine a man's attitude and direction of purpose. The moment spent by a marksman in taking his aim determines the whole course of his bullet.

(*c*) Except for the passage named, there is absolutely no support in Scripture for this theory. And even this passage is so obscure and uncertain in its meaning that we dare not balance it against the great mass of Scripture teaching, e.g., Luke xvi. 26. Out of dozens of interpretations that have been suggested, it is quite as likely that it means that Christ, in the person of Noah, proclaimed His message to the wicked of that day, who are now " spirits in prison," as that it means that Christ Himself went and preached to them in the interval between His Death and Resurrection.

(*d*) If the probation of this life does not suffice, why should a second one suffice? May not a third, and a fourth, and, in fact, an indefinite number be needed?

(*e*) The Bible throughout concentrates all its exhortations into the present: the burden of its message is, " To-day, while it is called to-day, harden not your hearts " (cf. Heb. iii. 12-15).

(*iii*) *Annihilation of the Wicked*

The theory of the *Annihilation of the Wicked* supposes that punishment will take the form of annihilation, or extinction. Such support as it finds in Scripture is drawn from a crudely literal interpretation of certain passages which speak of " destruction " as the destiny of the wicked, e.g., Matt. vii. 13 ; Phil. iii. 19 ; 2 Thess. i. 9 ; 2 Peter ii. 1. But apart from the mass of Scripture which points to the *conscious* suffering of the wicked, destruction is not the same as annihilation: a ship is destroyed when it is wrecked, and a house when it falls in ruins, but they are not actually annihilated.

(iv) Conditional Immortality

The theory of *Conditional Immortality* argues that Christ has " brought life and incorruption to light " (2 Tim. i. 10), and that eternal life is only " in Christ," so that those who are not " in Christ " simply perish.   At first sight there appear to be numerous passages of Scripture which point in this direction, e.g., John iii. 36, v. 24, x. 28, xvii. 2 and 3 ; Rom. vi. 23 ; 1 John v. 11.

The *objections* are, however, sufficiently serious to make it the least tenable of the theories.

(1) It has to deny that natural immortality of man, which as we saw on pp. 103—106, is an essential part of our belief concerning him, and which is almost instinctive throughout the race.   It is true that the Bible nowhere labours to prove man's immortality, but the New Testament throughout appears to take it for granted.

(2) The theory logically involves the conclusion that the wicked finally cease to exist at death, for, if man is not naturally immortal, it is impossible to see how he can survive even until the Resurrection and the Judgment. Yet Scripture asserts emphatically that there is a Resurrection and a Judgment of the wicked (John v. 29, etc.).

(3) The theory rests on a manifestly false interpretation of the words " life in Christ," for they certainly do not mean continuance of existence but a certain kind of spiritual condition.   " Life " in this sense is something that men may possess now, over and above their human existence (Col. iii. 3; 1 John iii. 14, v. 13).

(4) Similarly, the " death " spoken of as the punishment of sin (Rom. vi. 23) is not cessation of being, for many who were still living were described by St. Paul as dead in trespasses and sins (Eph. ii. 1).   If the consequence of sin was cessation of being, we should expect to see the beginning of this here.   It is true that certain vices may lead to physical ruin and death, but this is not true of sin

generally. The wicked are not generally feebler in body, mind, or will because of their sin: a bad man may be as resolute and as mentally acute in evil as the good man is in good. The " death " which is the penalty of sin is the death of the nobler powers and instincts.

(v) Eternal Punishment

The only alternative that remains is what is known by the terrible name of *Eternal Punishment*. Most of the *objections* to it have been noticed and dealt with in the treatment of the other theories, but they may be summed up here.

(1) Endless punishment seems both incredibly cruel and incredibly useless. But this is only the case if we regard it as positive and vindictive torment, not if we regard it as the natural working out of sin and its consequences.

(2) It seems to leave God's victory and sovereignty incomplete. It will be a disappointment of His hope, but, so long as man is free, that must always be a possibility. Yet God's sovereignty will not be incomplete, for all will acknowledge it, though some may not submit to it.

(3) It seems unjust that infinite issues should be determined by so short a life. But it is not unjust if men are judged according to their opportunities ; and especially if they are judged by the aim and direction of their life, rather than by its actual doings.

(4) Two or three passages seem to promise that all will be saved, e.g., John vi. 37 ; 1 Tim. ii. 4. But they have to be interpreted in the light of the great mass of New Testament teaching, and so indicate a purpose of God which man's free will may partially frustrate.

It is only with great reluctance that any one can come to accept this awful doctrine, but the *reasons for believing it* are as follows:

(1) No other theory is really satisfactory or consistent with Scripture. None of them can be maintained except by ignoring many passages and perverting others. We

cannot, perhaps, quite escape the feeling that on this matter the New Testament writers do not entirely agree with one another, or even with themselves—that can hardly surprise us considering the dark obscurity of the whole subject. Yet there is no question that an unbiased reader, making acquaintance with the New Testament for the first time, would conclude that the natural meaning of its teaching on this subject is Eternal Punishment.

(2) The following passages amongst many others leave us no option: Matt xxv. 46 ; Luke xvi. 26 ; 2 Thess. i. 9. It is sometimes urged that the Greek word *aionios* does not necessarily mean " endless," but only " age-long," or " very, very long." It is quite true that it means " as long as the age," and so may be interpreted, " as far into the future as our thought can carry us." But whilst, therefore, it does not specifically say that the punishment of the wicked will have no end, there is little comfort in that: for it does mean that it will have no end within any period of which we can conceive. The word is the nearest approach to " eternal " that Greek possessed, and it had to be used as the only word possible, to describe the bliss of the righteous as well as the woe of the wicked (see Matt. xxv. 46). It should be remembered, however, that in a spiritual existence Time has no meaning, and life is not measured out in days and years. Compare what was said about the eternity of God's existence on pages 29, 30.

The one thought of comfort in the whole matter is that men are in the hands of a God of Holiness and Love. The doctrine was taught, not in stern Old Testament days, but as part of the Gospel or the Good News ; and it was taught emphatically by Jesus Christ Himself (see Matt. xviii. 8, 9 ; xxv. 46, etc.). If the Master found no difficulty in reconciling it with the Goodness and the Love of God, we, too, may rest in the belief that the Judge of all the earth will do right ; and feel assured that, whatever the doom of the wicked may be, it will be one that commends itself to the tender heart of Jesus, to the righteous, and to the wicked themselves, as right and just.

Further, we have no right to suppose that the number

who are lost will necessarily be large. Our Lord refused to answer a question on this subject (Luke xiii. 23) ; but we do know that the number of the saved will so far exceed the number of the lost, that " He shall see of the travail of His soul and shall be satisfied " (Isa. liii. 11).

F.—THE BLISS OF THE RIGHTEOUS

A spiritual world. Much of what was said on pp. 170, 171, as to the general conditions of life in a spiritual world applies to Heaven as well as to Hell. The rich and luxuriant descriptions of its glory given in the Book of the Revelation (e.g., Rev. xxi 10-27) are obviously figurative, and must be interpreted accordingly. Also Heaven, like Hell, is a community of kindred spirits, and only secondarily a place.

The doctrine of Heaven has suffered to some extent from the tendency to speak of the bliss of the Future as a *reward,* and Christian people have sometimes laid themselves open to the charge that their virtue is self-seeking, and has for its only aim the winning of Heaven, as if it were a kind of prize. But if we were right in supposing that the woe of the wicked consists chiefly in the natural unfolding of sin and its consequences, in a world where the present restraints are removed, we must also suppose that the chief blessedness of Heaven consists in the further development of the good that is within us, under conditions much more favourable to goodness than those which surround us here ; and the desire for such a Heaven is not an unworthy motive, for only the man who really loves goodness will desire it.

General Characteristics of the Heavenly Life

Stripping away the imagery of the highly figurative descriptions of the Future given in the Revelation, and comparing them with simpler and more direct statements in the Epistles, we find several important and suggestive ideas which constitute the real teaching of the New Testament concerning the life of Heaven.

(1) Most of what we know may be summed up in the

fact that the righteous will be *with Christ* (Phil. i. 23 ;
1 Thess. iv. 17).   Hence many are content to say:

> My knowledge of that life is small,
>   The eye of faith is dim ;
> But 'tis enough that Christ knows all,
>   And I shall be with Him.

But to be with Christ involves certain necessary
consequences:

(*a*) *Likeness to Him.*   For St. John this is the inevitable
result of seeing Him " as He is " (1 John iii. 2).

(*b*) *Perfect knowledge* of spiritual and unseen things.
For St. Paul the most interesting consequence is that we
shall no longer " know in part " (1 Cor. xiii. 12).   This
implies the dissipation of our doubts, our perplexities, our
ignorance concerning God, and our misunderstanding of
His dealings with us.   One aspect of this fuller knowledge
is set forth in the words:

> Then shall I hear, and see, and know
> All I desired and wished below.

Another aspect of it is described in the words of another
favourite hymn:

> I'll bless the hand that guided,
>   I'll bless the heart that planned,
> When throned where glory dwelleth
>   In Immanuel's land.

(2) The next important feature of the heavenly life is
that it will mean *deliverance from material conditions.*
Under this we may include:

(*a*) Deliverance from what is sometimes described as
" *the burden of the flesh,*" i.e., deliverance from the
wants, the weariness, the sickness, the pain, and the animal
appetites that belong to the flesh.

(*b*) Escape from those *restrictions and limitations* of
the earthly life by which we are so often cramped and
baffled in our aspirations ; for there can be few who are

not sometimes conscious of being " cabin'd, cribb'd, confined, bound in " by earthly conditions which prevent them from realizing the more spacious and abundant life for which they long.

(*c*) Escape from the *transient,* the *changing,* and the *disappointing ;* for " the things which are seen are temporal, but the things which are not seen are eternal " (2 Cor. iv. 18). Amongst other things this includes the end of all that *sorrow* of parting and of bereavement, and the end of that *fear* and uncertainty about the morrow, which all must experience in a changing world like this.

(3) *Freedom from Sin.* For those who are deeply conscious of their frailty and shortcoming, there is nothing more inspiring in the promise of the Future than the knowledge that the *struggle with sin* will then be over.

(*a*) The daily battle with *temptation* will be ended, for there will be no evil influences around us to arouse sinful desires.

(*b*) The *holiness* to which the good aspire will be perfected, not in the sense that there will be no further moral progress and expansion possible, but in the sense that our nature will be wholly pure and good (cf. Rev. vii. 14).

(4) Scripture has much to say of the *glory* of the future life. It is, of course, almost as impossible for us to conceive what this means as it would be for the grub to conceive of the ampler and more glorious life into which it will some day enter as a butterfly (cf. 1 Cor. ii. 9). But some faint parallel may be found in the change experienced by a man of intellectual aspirations and artistic tastes who passes suddenly from the sordid surroundings and laborious toil of poverty into the life of ease, leisure, refinement and travel, that is made possible by the acquisition of wealth.

(5) A feature of the heavenly life which has been less prominent in the popular conception of the Future than it ought to be is *endless progress,* both in moral development and in the knowledge of God. This is suggested by

our Saviour's statement, " This is life eternal, that they should be *getting to know* Thee the only true God, and Him whom Thou didst send, even Jesus Christ " (John xvii. 3) ; for the word He uses means to " get to know " rather than " to know." This knowledge of God is never exhausted. Similarly, St. Paul describes the love of God as something which " passeth knowledge " (Eph. iii. 19). The same idea is expressed in the words:

> But, Oh, eternity's too short
> To utter all Thy praise.

Similarly, we can set no limit to the progress that may be possible in thought, in mental and spiritual capacity, and in knowledge of that glorified Universe.

This idea of progress makes a strong appeal to the modern mind, since it links the life of the future onto the life of the present, and makes it a continuation of the evolution and development which have characterized the history of the Universe in the past.

(6) Another idea which has been to some extent over-looked is that of *larger and wider service for God*. It is the burden of our Saviour's teaching in the parable of the Talents (Matt. xxv. 14-30) that the reward of faithful service is larger opportunities of service beyond. Cf. also the words, " His servants shall do Him service " (Rev. xxii. 3). The tendency has often been to regard Heaven merely as a place of rest, or to represent its everlasting praise as consisting in the service of song rather than in the service of active devotion. But many for whom the former conception of Heaven has little attraction, are attracted by the idea of larger powers and wider activities in God's work. What form that service for Him may take, it is impossible to say. Tennyson has exquisitely described it as a life of great enterprise,

> In such high offices as suit
> The full-grown energies of heaven ;

and everything points to the fact that it will be work exactly adapted to our capacity and inclination ; work in which we shall find delight ; work in which there will be neither the irksomeness, the weariness, nor the sense of failure and inefficiency, that we so often experience here. To complete a quotation which was made in part above:

> Then shall I see, and hear, and know
> All I desired and wished below ;
> And every power find sweet employ
> In that eternal world of joy.

It is impossible to read the great words " to the ages of the ages " without the vision of the successive ages that make up Eternity unfolding themselves in orderly and consecutive progress, and involving a continuous and unbroken work of God in which we may have a share.

G.—THE CONSUMMATION OF ALL THINGS

Christ as King. Beyond what it has to say of the destiny of men in the Future, the New Testament throws out some hints concerning these great and solemn events as they will affect the Divine Being. As regards the Saviour, it points to a gathering up of all things into one in Him (Eph. i. 10), sometimes known as the *Consummation of all things in Christ.* Much the same idea is expressed more simply in the statement of St. Paul that every knee shall bow and every tongue confess that Jesus Christ is Lord (Phil. ii. 10) ; and also in the great chorus of Rev. xi. 15:

" The Kingdom of the world is become the kingdom of our Lord and of His Christ:

AND HE SHALL REIGN FOR EVER AND EVER."

God All in All. The teaching of St. Paul in 1 Cor. xv. 24-28 carries us yet a stage further. The passage is difficult, but it appears to mean that Christ will then have perfected that Kingdom of the Redeemed, which He, as the Incarnate Son, came to prepare, and in which up to that point He will be supreme. But having prepared it to be " the Kingdom of *God,*" He will then resign the Sovereignty to God, even the Father ; though He Himself will still share in the Sovereignty as one Person in the Triune God. The words of St. Paul are:

" And when all things have been subjected unto Him, then shall the Son also Himself be subjected to Him that did subject all things unto Him,

THAT GOD MAY BE ALL IN ALL."

Thus our study, which began with the Sovereignty of God, ends where it began, with this difference, that it shows us that Sovereignty extended to include Mankind as God's free and willing servants, a Sovereignty achieved in spite of their Rebellion and Sin, and a Sovereignty achieved by Love.

Christian Theology has been described as " A beautiful system, even though it does include the Fall." And so it is, for it forms a complete and consistent whole, and is a noble scheme of thought, with only such incompleteness and mystery attending it as necessarily belong to all the knowledge of finite human minds.

But Christian Theology is far more than a scheme of thought, however noble or fascinating: it has a great practical end in view:

" These (things) are written, that ye may *believe* that Jesus is the Christ, the Son of God ; and that believing ye may *have life* in His name " (John xx. 31).

UNTO HIM THAT LOVETH US, AND LOOSED US FROM OUR SINS BY HIS BLOOD ; AND HE MADE US TO BE A KINGDOM, TO BE PRIESTS UNTO HIS GOD AND FATHER ; TO HIM BE THE GLORY AND THE DOMINION FOR EVER AND EVER. AMEN.

Rev. i. 5, 6.

INDEX

NOTES

NOTES

NOTES